APOCALYPSE EMERGENCY

Also by Michael Adzema

From the Return to Grace series

Culture War, Class War. Volume 1
Apocalypse NO. Volume 4
Experience Is Divinity. Volume 8

Wounded Deer and Centaurs. Volume 5 (forthcoming)
The Great Reveal by the Planetmates. Volume 6 (forthcoming)
Funny God. Volume 7 (forthcoming)
Falls from Grace. Volume 9 (forthcoming)
Primal Return. Volume 10 (forthcoming)

APOCALYPSE EMERGENCY

Love's Wake-Up Call

Return to Grace, Volume 3

MICHAEL ADZEMA

To all those who have dedicated and sacrificed their lives to save the life on this planet.

CONTENTS

ACKNOWLEDGMENTS

I wish to acknowledge the invaluable love and support of my wife, Mary Lynn Adzema. Truly we have shared our thoughts and feelings in the creation and inspiration of everything I write. Who but the most stalwart and worthy, or mad, would journey with this mind of mine?

I want to mention the inspiration I have received from my goddaughter, Elizabeth, and my nephew, Tim. Their innocence, laughter, and love were constant reminders to me of what we are fighting for, as I was writing this book. If I work too hard, as some people are wont to say, well … thinking of the children and the world we are leaving them … I know I have damn good reason to.

CHAPTER 1

SEVEN BILLION NEROS FIDDLING

IT'S A TRILLION-ALARM FIRE, NOT A BOY SCOUT LITTER CAMPAIGN

A Trillion-Alarm Fire — You Don't Stop at the Grocery on Your Way Home!

I compare what is happening right now to cause planetary death in the relatively near future to a trillion-alarm fire with everyone looking the other way. I say you need to respond to this with the urgency of being in a world war, marshaling all available national and world resources to bear on it, and not with the complacency of a boy-scout litter pick-up campaign.

When you get a call at work that your house is on fire, you rush home worrying about whether your family is alive or dead, what, if anything, remains of your precious keepsakes, and so on. And you don't, this time, stop on the way to have a short visit with your mother at the nursing home, grab a few things at the grocery store, or even fill up your tank at the gas station! *You go straight home and try to save your family and home!*

What follows, from May of 2010, is an example of the attitude of dealing with global apocalyptic events as if, like in this case, they are of similar importance to a plane going down. My point, of course, is that we should be dealing with them with all the urgency of a "trillion-alarm fire" happening. For each of these are disasters contributing to an ongoing catastrophic ecocidal process, the tip of which, only, we see in the Fukushima reactor blowups and the Gulf Oil Spill:

Matthews: "four-alarm fire" in Gulf! Landrieu smirks. Matthews: There are ways to suck up oil ... it is a US emergency not just a BP business problem

May 25, 2010. Today, Chris Matthews likened the Gulf Oil Spill to a four-alarm fire. While Senator Mary Landrieu smirked, Matthews said, "I don't know what the legality of this is, but the President of the United States has got this challenge, not just BP. BP has got a business challenge; we have a national challenge. North America that we inherited and would like to pass on to our future generations is in big trouble."

Earlier, in answer to a question by Matthews as to whether there's "anybody in the world that can come and collect petroleum ... that's out there in the Gulf right now ... anybody that can collect it?" Landrieu responded saying, "Well, first of all, Chris, just let me say this: If Delta Airlines ... plane goes down, I don't think we necessarily call all the airlines to come in and help in this very specific way. Now, I will tell you, that all the oil companies have been helping since day one, informally...."

Are you as concerned as I am hearing that kind of cavalier attitude about human life?

Oil Spills and Reactor Blowups

"Where Is the Fierce Urgency of Now?!!!"

I can't believe the nonchalance around the huge environmental catastrophes that have gone on in just the last few years alone — specifically, the Gulf Oil Spill and the Fukushima Japan nuclear disaster. When the BP disaster was ongoing and gushing devastating amounts of oil into the Gulf, Donna Brazille, frustrated with the Obama Administration's response to the Spill, fumed aloud, "Where is the fierce urgency of Now?!!!"

But these hugely unprecedented environmental catastrophes, daily spreading the damage to our planet, are just two canaries in a coal mine.

We are just beginning to understand the immensity of the damage to our planet the Fukushima disaster did. We will probably not be told the degree of radiation exposure from it we are receiving until long after people have been dying in droves from it.

The BP oil spill of 2010 is, similarly, presenting ongoing planetary damage, which, like the Japan nuclear disaster, is, as I speak, not being reported. Dolphin and whale carcasses in the hundreds have been washing up on Gulf beaches, birds have been dying and some are simply dropping dead out of the sky. We know for sure of at least one dead zone caused by the BP oil spill — a dead zone being an area in the ocean where nothing can live for lack of oxygen — which is a hundred miles long and twelve miles wide. I have heard reports of other dead zones cropping up in the Gulf, and it has been said they are *growing* in size with time. Beyond these we have to wonder how many more there are, yet unknown, and how great is the ongoing damage.

But none of these dire events are being mentioned much in the media. We hear the reports, but then the media directs our attention to something else. When Fukushima was being actively monitored by the media in 2011, I heard CNN report some very apocalyptic developments occurring there. Immediately afterward, CNN directed our attention to some in-depth reporting on a snake that had gotten loose in New York City. Now that snake made me sooo scared, I don't know why!? *sarcasm*

So we cover our eyes to what is going on. *sigh*

We dismiss these events assuming that someone higher up than us is surely attending to the problem (dream on!). Though we would never admit it, we take comfort in thinking that people more in the know and influential — people with more status, degrees, power — are on the front line and will certainly make better decisions than we ever could. So doing, we blind ourselves to the fact that these people in charge are blinded and made stupid by their greed and self-interest. They see dimly, if at all, through that screen at the dire prospects they are juggling with. With such tunnel vision, they are hardly capable of seeing the interests of humanity, let alone acting on them. Furthermore, they console themselves with the thought that someone else higher up — or not, often just someone *other* than them — is "certainly" taking care of "the big things."

Ultimately, people are passing the buck ALL the way up … to God. Seriously, this theological cul-de-sac is the ultimate, most reliable, place of retreat for the theistic as well as most of the non-theistic, if people were to be honest about their thoughts. But this is the most comforting of cop-outs and the greatest excuse to carry on acting recklessly out of all-too-trivial motivations of unhinged greed and blind self-interest.

What is worse is these things are only the tiny beginnings of much more that is bound to happen. If we do not listen up, and wake up, we'll be just as unprepared and helpless when the even more dire and apocalyptic events unfold. This is not a time to curl up under the covers.

Die-Off of 250 Million Species in Under Fifty Years ... And You Really Think We'll Be Here?

OR, Have You Heard the New Version of the 12 Days of Christmas? It Ends With "7 Billion Nero's Fiddling." But No One Lives Long Enough to Finish It ... Ever.

Scientists are saying we will see a fifty percent die-off rate, extinction, of species within the next twenty to fifty years. That is to say, within that time half the species we see now — well actually about five years ago — will be gone forever.[1]

To think that we will be around after that, even to watch video games of the wildlife that once was, is the same as a doctor saying to someone: "Sorry, within twenty to fifty years, half of the organs in your body will be gone. They'll die and 'fall' away, and you'll be DISABLED."

Would such a person just be *disabled!?* Do you get my point?

You see, you tell me how we're going to be alive to even see what happens after that kind of extinction?! Does no one realize how much death that means? Does no one see any interconnections between us and planetmates? The world will come to an end if bankers don't get money, they told Americans in 2008. And if they did away with roads, or trucks ... it's Mad Max time, right? Well, how about when the bees didn't show up? One species out of a scientifically estimated five-hundred million species and our economy was going ape shit! What happens with two-hundred-fifty MILLION species gone forever?!

Ecocide

Global, Universal Death/Extinction Isn't Just Death, Suicide; It Is MURDER, Of a Kind So Evil, Nazis Look Like Mother Theresas by Comparison

Concerning extinction of species — ourselves and other species — which is going on, an idea was put forth to me that we are assuming death is evil. This person intended, considering the context, for this to be taken spiritually, philosophically.

Re: The Psychology of Extinction: Murder of untold billions through greed, laziness, egotism....Well, I say, EVIL!

My reply was: You make the point that needs to be considered as it sits deep down in the hidden center of this particular wordpool. It's a mind-bender and mind-stretcher when you stray down your road for sure. But after having been down it a fair number of times, both on my own as well as with companions, I find one tangible, unshakable thing, only, to still and focus my vision and guide my stance, actions, and position with surety. It is this:

I, for one, am not assuming death is an evil. I do not believe death is evil at all, quite the contrary. Death has always been a part of life, and all the religions have it as a sublime culmination of a life well lived. But that is a spiritual perspective. And that is a perspective about death in its essence.

It is a vision from a spiritual stance — rooted in science, philosophy, and Eastern mysticism — as well as from a traditional religious view, where it is held that one's life in the body is only a try-out for a better, "real" life in "heaven."[2]

However, you are mistaking, as analogy, the beautiful precise utility of a finely honed and balanced knife — metaphorically speaking — with what is really important and what is so hard to look at or fathom or even let into one's thoughts: That is

... the horrific, ghastly, unbelievably bloody and messy, grotesque, garish ... infinitely hellacious and mind-drippingly insane ... scene that is right in front of all of us: that of the angelic young girl and her vulnerable, innocent, and kind-hearted mother, their bodies slashed, cut up, stabbed, gouged, even chopped and minced, and strewn widely and randomly in this ungodly lake of blood framed within this just recently homey, comforting surround of simple comfortable living room furniture and accouterments, which now, however, are awash and stained and forever nightmarish as they record in blood, guts, and other of that ilk, but of which we do not want even to know, the violence, wild aggression, horrible pain, fear, terror, and trauma of the event — the murder ... the murder that was so precisely perfect in its nightmarishness as it was aided in its perfect horror ...

by such a beautifully crafted, finely honed, exquisitely and marvelously sharp, perfectly balanced and joyous to feel, hold, and use knife.

What I am saying is, OK death is beautiful, in essence. And going back to God is, my belief, the highest accomplishment and culmination of a life lived well. But we are not talking about my death or your death. We are talking about you and I deciding, by refusing to fight back the apocalypse — which could be taken up merely by changing some of our greedy, wasteful, egoistic ways — the death of untold trillions of other living conscious beings, indeed, of conscious things that we are not evolved enough to even be aware of. We are deciding that THEIR death, because of our actions ... well, that's not so evil, eh?

Well, that's easy for *us* to say. But how about them? Don't you think they might be a tad upset that we would be deciding this FOR THEM ... (Jonestown-style)?

So, you bring up the point that needs to be addressed before we can really commit ourselves to the fight and the struggle to change that is being required of us. But I offer that I have never found anyone able to shake or even threaten the principle I have found to stand on: God's creation, which includes death, in Her (His) time and in the way He (She) would have for each of us, is beauteous perfection. But, MURDER ... that is, MY deciding ... or ANYONE (but God) deciding for another that death is good, well ... well ... Is not that what Hitler did? What the Nazis did?

Death — not evil — may be beautiful.

Murder of untold multi-billion-trillions through greed, laziness, egotism, hubris, and extreme lack of empathy and feeling for the feelings/consciousness of those others ... well, I say,

EVIL!!!

Evil beyond all imagining. Evil beyond anything ever conceived or acted ever before in the billions of years of existence of this planet.

EVIL! Even the killing of the planet — its systems so perfectly balanced, so far beyond our understanding — of a Nature that is beyond our comprehension, which, for all we know, is akin to a higher consciousness, a deva, a god, goddess.

Yes, EVIL to murder. Incredibly evil to bring to an end such things so far above and beyond our understanding that we cannot even comprehend the magnitude of that evil.

Now, that is my conclusion. I deem that murder on a scale so huge as to be inconceivable, of numbers of beings so great we have no way of knowing the hideous magnitude of the crime, not to mention seven billion alone of our own species, and laying to waste the dreams, efforts, and results of multibijillions of past lives on this planet of all species IS EVIL!

That is something I do not want to ever think I helped to happen.... Indeed it is EVIL so huge that I think I would not feel right, ever again, in the consciousness forever after this life and after my death, if I did not expend every ounce of my energy while I still can/could to try to prevent, to try to stop, to work against, to struggle to keep it from happening.

I think that consciousness cannot be destroyed — so death is not "evil." But as we stand on the precipice of this planet murder and hugest crime of all time as far as we know before us and with us, as a species, being the cause of it.... Well, I can only say the worst thing that I can imagine is having an eternity of consciousness knowing that I could have been part of the solution, but I trivialized it. I used a convenient spiritual belief/ teaching/ awareness to rationalize it so that I could continue asleep and unaware of the horror I participated in as I chose, through being afraid to look at the immense suffering involved, to blind myself with distractions — the perfect knife, the death that is not evil. And so instead of an eternity of peace knowing that I stood against the greatest evil ever known and fought as hard as I could, although we failed ... instead it could be an eternity of regret and loathing not being able to be unaware that I was a part of the horror, the monster, participated in the killing, and helped others to also, by participating in the feel-good cover-up, the blinding of eyes, the zombification of brains. As the deepest darkness ever known gradually but unmistakably arose on the horizon and came toward us, increasing in speed, becoming more fiercesome, detailed, clear, unmistakable, unavoidable, and ever harder to be blind to, ever clearer in its brutality and the suffering, and unimaginable pain in its aftermath. And so I would spend an eternity knowing, not being able to not know, that I WAS it, that I became it, helped it ... that I was, er, "part of the problem" ... and I didn't have to be.

And for everyone else I would ask: Care to choose what you'd like to have sitting around in that imperishable unending forever consciousness we're "blessed" with?

The End of the World

A correspondent of mine emailed me to recommend a book by John Leslie titled, *The End of the World*.

More People Living Now Than the Grand Total of Humans Who Have Ever Lived!

She said the book makes a disturbingly solid case for our extinction, saying that we are among the last generations of humans. Part of this reasoning involves a complex mathematical determination of our trajectory, which includes the interesting calculation that there are twice as many humans alive, right now, THAN THE GRAND TOTAL OF HUMANS THAT HAVE EVER LIVED. That last is a provocative finding, to say the least.

Now, I haven't read the book, but just his premise got me to thinking. Of course, what I know confirms his conclusions in spades, but I couldn't help feeling irked by his all-too-familiar perspective. For, to me, it is not just about our species. It is not just about our extinction. It is not just suicide, but murder. My correspondent, "Open Intelligence," has used the term, "ecocide," to make this kind of point.

Ok We're Committing Species-Suicide; But How DARE We Become Species-Suicide-Bombers Killing All OTHER Life With Us

Recently, I checked on the actual number of species that currently are on our planet, and the number was estimated at five-hundred million SPECIES. I think the whole problem IS that we only see "life" in terms of "our" life — our species. Indeed, some people think in terms of life being only for those of their religion, nation, social group, tribe, family, or even just oneself — all of which aid the murder of those who are "not life."

So, Leslie is apparently thinking along the lines of many others who are not seeing the tragedy we are perpetrating to those other than our species, which is a milder form of the bigotry and prejudice we hold for one human against another type of human. I think that is a shame.[3]

But then we cannot seem to even wake people up to saving themselves or their children, so how can we get them to empathize with the trillions upon trillions of other lives and the multi-hundred-millions of other life forms we share this planet with?

I guess that is my problem with his approach: It comes from my feeling that — Ok, we are committing suicide, but maybe we fucking deserve it. But how DARE we "blow up" — like a species suicide bomber — without a second thought for their pain or their lives — which we are only too dumb, and ego- species-centric, bigoted to see, let alone empathize with — as simple "collateral damage," innumerable multi-bijilliion-trillions of innocent souls/ life forms and hundreds of millions of other entire species of them with us. That is murder of the highest degree, and an evil that this planet has never imagined before this time.

But, again, I see the point of talking to people where they are coming from as a starting point, as Leslie is doing. But shouldn't we try to raise as much awareness as possible of, to me, the much greater evil that we are committing, for those who can hear it? I say, if we want to kill ourselves off, fine. But how dare we sink to becoming the biggest mass murderers of all time, by a multi-multi-trillionfold? We are currently making the Nazis look like Mother Theresas by comparison. If there will be a history of our species by an alien race after we are gone, I do not doubt that the words "Fukushima" and "Oil Spill dead zones," will have the same kind of black potency that "Auschwitz" and "Dachau" currently have for us.

Suicidal Apes and Our Future as Mars

If you care about your children, you'll "man up," "woman up," "cowboy up," whatever … anything but cover up … and face the horror, become the noble humans we are capable of being, and join with others to pull off the most heroic actions of all time.…

Or else we'll be deemed throughout the Universe as "suicidal ape," and our portrait will be no different from Mars.

The better angels of our beings urge us to pay attention to what is being said in the writing below.

Consider the Topic and then that By the Ending I Was Feeling Euphoric,
Having Just Stared Deeply Into the Most Horrible Likely Future Conceivable.

MEANING:

Either you really should be checking this out...
Or I Should Be Getting Checked Out... but seriously, folks...

Now you'd THINK this would be a morose piece. I am the author of "Love's Wake-Up Call, Apocalypse Emergency" — which is the chapter coming up — and I fully expected this to be a call to awareness that only the brave or the Goths would listen to. But honestly, I confess that the writing that came out of me and that I then expanded upon further in the reading over of it afterward was beautiful and led to a conclusion that inspired me (that's not supposed to happen!) and left me feeling calmer than I have been for a long time.

What's in It?

Ok, Ok, so you want to know what's in this wake-up call? I'm tempted to say "grab bag" and split, figuring to let Higher Power decide who gets to read this. Sure this is in me; but there is more here than I, well at least thought, was in me.

No, I'll give you the poop: It's about a frightening global predicament that everyone seems to be aware of, but which few people are giving the attention and seriousness it deserves. I liken it to a thousand-alarm fire going off right now, with everyone looking away. I talk about why people would do that, why the media would be inclined to shy away. Basically it's understandable because we simply have no way of comprehending the magnitude of what is happening and how fast, since no living thing on this planet in its multibillion year history has had to face what we are.[4]

I Found Compassion, Not Blame.

I use spiritual fantasy and real world analogies to help us get a handle on what we're facing. In jumping into these waters, I expected to be emotionally beat up. Instead I came to many understandings and found I saw the positions of many who aren't helping right now somewhat through their eyes, and found compassion, not blame.

Now that I think of it, I am having the realization that the reason for my serene, compassionate, and loving feelings while doing this parallels why I felt there was hope in the end.

I realize that facing dire challenges — and this being the most dire of all — brings out the best in humans. It always has. Though this has been put off so long we might not do anything substantive till it's too late, I realize that a political change away from the George W. Bush debacle in Washington may be having unknown but positive ripple effects around the world. In essence, it is only since then that either Americans or those around the world can feel they can apply themselves to tackling this biggest of all challenges. For the Bush administration was disheartening and disillusioning to people of the globe who cared about the environmental crisis and of course to us in America as well. We could not help but feel that any efforts we could make would be quickly outswamped by the Republicans' massive anti-environmental policies ... sneakily disguised in environmentally positive sounding labels, though they were.

Not that everything has changed in America since Bush left office or that corporations are back on their heels in their attempts at thwarting our wills to life. No, it is a continual uphill slog. Still, when Bush was US president, it was utterly hopeless. It is very disheartening when your own government seems to consider your life completely expendable when it comes to short term gains for the Bushies — the corporate and "filthy rich" FOB's.

The Ending Lifted Me.

While the ending of this piece lifted me up in a way that I haven't felt in a long time on this matter, I must admit that my long term study of humans — as a depth psychotherapist and as a student of other cultures across all time periods, that is, anthropology — informed my conclusions, shaped them, and took me to visions of possible futures that I did not expect. They would seem, if not as likely, then at least as worthy of the human spirit as we deserve.

We'll Be Tested and Found Worthy … Or Deserving of Our Grave.

For all we've done it seems we have called down upon ourselves to be tested and to be found either worthy, or deserving of the grave we're digging.

The chapter coming up, "Love's Wake-Up Call," goes back and forth between these horrors that are possible and, well, let us say, this unique situation with the potential so strong to bring humans to raise themselves up and be led by their better angels more than any other time. What it will mean could be exciting and triumphant beyond belief as humans come out of their puerile adolescent phase and become united and shaped for millennia by this great struggle. We could also die trying our mightiest, which has a nobility to it.

Currently we are looking like the stupidest beings ever to dream the dream of thingness and duality.

It'll be scary and interesting, and you'll be helped if you have a strong faith in a Higher Power.

Beyond that, it will be the biggest adventure that the entire globe ever faced together, and the outcome could be just about anything.

Reversing Babel

But don't get the popcorn, you won't be sitting for this one; no one will. Indeed, if we succeed, we will look back at such terms as "couch potato" and wonder at the lost, unfulfilled lives they describe, which will seem a strange thing in a future that will require all of us to come together in a way that we haven't seen since before — metaphorically speaking of course — The Tower of Babel.

So while the odds will be against us and even certain segments of humanity will try to monkey wrench our positive efforts, success could be wondrous beyond all belief.

I've said too much. The piece is complete in itself, and if you dare, you may find yourself strangely invigorated. At least I hope you get some, if not a lot, of the benefits and positive attitude adjustment that I received.

"We're All in This Together."

I left the piece feeling so much love and unity with all humans and living things, for I knew that at no other time in the history of the world was the truth of the saying "we're all in this together" more patently true.

CHAPTER 2

LOVE'S WAKE-UP CALL

APOCALYPSE EMERGENCY

There are topics you will rarely if ever hear in the mainstream media. It is not that they are not true; it is that these true things are ... well ... is there such a thing as too true? Truth that the vast majority of people will either not hear, or will distort, will deny, will conveniently find hard to understand — that is, they will retreat into confusion — and so many other things? Obviously, by the title, you already know the kinds of truths I'm referring to.

Your Child Will Die, How Can You Turn Away?

Our species has never been confronted with such truths — facts about the inevitable demise of our entire species in short order, unless something on a massive scale is done. And it seems our systems have no capacity for it. For indeed such an event has never occurred on our planet in its entire multibillion year history.

So the fact you are even reading this, fully aware of the title, proves you are one of the few who are opting to know the truth — however disturbing — rather than turn your head, as an unbelievable number of people are currently doing, to the *likelihood* of apocalypse…. Sorry, that's not something people want to know. But ecocide, planet death, apocalypse will be a certainty unless people get the courage to do something, which necessarily of course starts with LOOKING at the problem!

OK, I'll try again, this isn't easy for me either….

The cumulative scientific evidence relating to the fate of this planet has been accelerating in the direction of there being little to no hope that there will be much, if any, life on this planet, at some point only twenty to fifty years from now. So as I was trying to say above, many people are currently turning their head to the likelihood that we will all be dead in what will probably seem the fastest decades ever.

What makes this likelihood so disturbing is that many people know this and yet don't care. Some even get a charged up thrill, or sense of power at the prospect. And many others just can't wait! Sadly they have certain misguided religious beliefs — for example, "the rapture" — that have rationalized and made desirable this most abominable thing — wiping out the efforts and strivings and occurrences of billions of years and almost seven billion human souls alone in current time, and negating the passionate struggles of billions of humans prior to us who wanted more than anything else to leave the world a better place. But take a cynical — maddened — generation or two, and they may as well never have lived.

Why am I saying this? If you have children, or grandchildren, even if you might not see it, what kinds of parents exist now that blithely turn away from the trillion-alarm fire that is already waging, which will consume their beloveds in ways too horrible to contemplate? I do not understand it; for in any other situation where they would be threatened, wouldn't many even risk their own lives?

I need to say this because, despite the madness surrounding us in the minds of people stressed with problems of all kinds that are now at unprecedented levels, I have faith in God and in the nobility of humans at their base. I believe that more and more will not only face this horrible darker-than-night cloud looming and rushing us from the horizon, but will deem it to be the one worthy thing left to do, whichever way it goes. I am using my God-given skills of communication and intellect, along with a lifetime of study into the human mind and its healing, to try to reverse our current plunge.[1]

I know there are others like myself right now attempting to wake up the noble spirited, the heroic among us, who, once convinced, will add whatever unique qualities God has blessed them to this once in a multibillions chance to be good, kind, brave, hard-working, sympathetic, heartful, strong, God-loving, life embracing, laughter-, song-, and children-loving humans again.

To be humans again, not greedy beasts of prey with green in their eyes and their blood, who have been taking over this planet for several decades now, for idiotically selfish ends. So maddened are they, we have already seen the first incredible detonation of their unconcern for this planet — all God's creatures on it, and even their own offspring — in this collapse of an entire global economic system in what seemed practically to be overnight in 2007. So insane they, we have seen the consequences of their greedy craving in the increasing radiation of the planet, through accidents like Fukushima, and the dying of the oceans — our oxygen source — with the Gulf Oil Spill.

So when I think the media is soft peddling this dire and vital truth of the approaching death of all as if providing the opium of pleasant reverie to a sick person, instead of providing the truth and giving the person the less pleasant and more strenuous options of fighting for one's health ... when I think of them as deciding for us, as if we are dying children, who they think they are being compassionate to when saying what amounts to "you're going to be just fine," and such, even as we, the children, take our last breath, I think of that syrupy mealy-mouthedness, that "comforting," as enabling us in an addiction and even covering up the suffering that might get us well. Taking a look at the media in this light, I am offended and feel disrespected. For I am not one who appreciates being pampered and protected from upset when it means that it will guarantee my death, do you?

For if a great many people do not quickly and radically reverse their lives — and no I'm not talking boy scout recycling efforts. I am talking about the gearing up and urgency that would need to be far greater than that of the last world war — how can it not be seen that the Nazi holocaust will seem a tea party alongside what's coming?

Unity Is Our Food Our Destination Our Bliss Our Home ...

But it is not warriors we need. That is part of the problem. We do need people as disciplined and caring, but not just of their buddies rather for all life, human and nonhuman, of all creation that God in His/Her great love for us and all life masterfully crafted, slowly, carefully, meticulously, over a near eternity this incredible planet, as finely balanced and perfect and precise, and wondrous and beautiful in infinite ways, precisely moving in perfect harmonious exquisite synchronicity of infinite living elements through the seasons, over the years, languorous and slow and allowing for a plenitude of experience, of possibilities for joyous play, exuberant and bountiful youthful sense of power, pride, belonging — for ALL creatures, and an infinite number of them — each of them single individuals sharing with us this possibility of joy, wonder, happiness, laughter, pain, grief, wisdom.... this divine adventure taken by so many humans even, each doing their best between the poles of the monstrous and the angelic, creating in the end, whatever the outcome, lives as different, as unique, as incomparable as any snowflake to another.

And all the while, surrounded from birth, breathing the divine. God always so close you can't see. But in every little thing pushing you to the exquisite slow, painful then wonderful unfolding into greater and greater wisdom, goodness, love, truthfulness and loving of truth — no matter how long it takes, or even lifetimes — slowly, slowly, turning, turning, expanding, flowing ever outward in wider and wider encompassing surrounds of wisdom and love — no matter how long it takes.

And on the way the dawnings of blissful openings of being, leaving the darkness of pain and ignorance more and more at our roots. Just as the lotus grows out of the muck of the dirty swamp, feeding on that muck for sustenance. Just as our hardships, mistakes, even our cruelties lead us in time that much more beautifully and committedly loving of love, of life, of goodness, of God. And our eyes ever more aware of the beauty always there but more and more radiant as the darkness slowly dissipates, and the lotus reaches its tender shoot higher and higher into the murky water. It too in time becoming increasingly aware of light that is above and that the darkness is more and more in behind it.

Until, just as we, there is that moment of arriving on the water surface and feeling and breathing, being free and so joyous, blissful, and understanding of the marvelous divine perfection of the experience, even when it seemed hopeless, just as we. And in gratitude and glory it unfolds its perfect, delicate pleasure in the expressions of joy that are the splendid beauteous aromatic creations that we call its many petals, but for the lotus is its song of gratitude. As much as our unfolding may open our hearts so deliciously loving and alive that we must sing to God, to Love, to the Consciousness that is the only Existing thing and equally coursing its wondrous way throughout all creation — lotus, human, in the loving ministrations of all God's creatures toward each other as we feel the attraction of like to like, of divine to divine....

And would this wonderful incredibly sweet sound of God's Life in us and around us, harmonizing over billions of years and to the ends of the Universe, the chorus of the divine, the harmony of the spheres, this grand, often dramatic and percussive symphony, the only reality, the only one really desired, the home of all whose sound is even telling you it is Om, where one belongs, where one loves and is loved and dualism-nondualism are irrelevant for equally delightful are the movements of this endless ever changing symphony, which must be separate and forgetful and also awake and one for the sheer beauty of it, for the sheer pleasure of remembering again the most wonderful truth of oneself, and then maybe again.

Of such possibilities and perceptions are the expanses outside, outside one's skin. As one's identity is not merely that within the gushing palpitation below the skin but expands to include spouse, family, children, others, all creatures, all beings known and unknown, with malice toward no one. As such unity is our food our destination our bliss our home....

Oh so sad and yet tender and beautiful and juicy we take our prodigal souls ever home. And more and more recognizing our brothers and sisters on the way, delighting in the exquisite separation that we will continue to enjoy until ready to release, to let go. Like a swimmer letting go of the side of the pool to sink deep into the crystal water, where it is then all the Universe that one experiences and then one becomes aware that one is just as much of it as in it.

And slowly delightfully then just not conceiving of any boundaries and the swimmer disappears to those still holding on to the delightful game of pretending that there is any such thing as a thing, as boundaries, as nations, as bodies.... Fun, that game of thingness ... for a while....

For it is just a game, a made up concocted set of parameters, boundaries, and rules. That we sit down on a pleasant Sunday afternoon to play, to enjoy the amazingly creative plays, humorous remarks, and outright belly-whomping creative utterances that our playmates entertain with and we enjoy also performing as things we do and say come so perfectly from, well … it's just there.

We just are, we can't help be, and whether irritated or laughing uproariously or snickering secretively as we plan our next play … in sweet anticipation of the reactions, surprise! befuddlement! or knowing smiles from another … it is all unknown and to be discovered.

So who would spoil such fun by ever letting on, even, or especially, to oneself that it is all known, there is no separation. Why we even might enjoy it more if we allow ourselves to suppose that the stakes are real — at which point we know we have taken the wondrous forgetfulness game of humanness. One only does that to enjoy the sweetest waking of all, that from the soundest and most undisturbed of all possible dreamings.

However you conceive it, though. You needn't buy my reverie. In fact how could you? Though you and I could be mirrors to each other it is the absolute knowing that we cannot be the same snowflake. No. You have your world, and your unique way of enjoying sweet existence.

Who Would Want Such an Ending to the Human Story? I'd Rather See People Becoming the Best Humans That Have Ever Lived on This Planet ….

But is it God's, yours, mine, anyone's plan that this multi-billion year sweet symphony of consciousness expressing itself as beauteous Nature is suddenly, in eternal time, within the last second or two, to be stomped, crackled, and crashed by the Caterpillar boots of newbie humans? The skin-bound ones. I mean, reaaalyy skin bound.

As for me such horrible catastrophic cacophony of destruction is about as creative and delight inducing as a slow wonderfully silent drive through a countryside in late spring. Fragrant, aromatic … feelings of gratitude to the All That Is. And hearts overflowing in appreciation of the company of such remarkable, loving, and brilliant of friends. So slowly meandering in fragrant meadows and moisty tart forests, one just regrets that the vehicle will have to stop to be charged in a little bit.

That's pleasant to me, maybe it is or isn't to you. But who among us would wish for the ride, the symphony, the song, the journey, the adventure, the whatever's finale to be a split second of angry irritation and then an all too easy wander off of the freeway home? Such that before one is even aware, oneself and one's friends and God's delightful chorus is composed … the ending, sixty miles per hour, six friends, the unmovable concrete of an overpass's supports kissing all six's bloody bags of water, water-balloon style erased on the slab.

And the percussive sounding to mark the end, over before you even realize it's begun. But when you in your awestruck wonder slow it to single frames, that sound … that sound so hideous, containing so many others within its one-second elapse. But you hear there are billions. You hear, trillions, more, infinite. Crashing, metal, but within it mixed … why, that is that hell that some speak about. All those voices crying out in loss, in anger:

"How have you the right?" "Why have you robbed…?" And all creatures that have ever lived here crying out in pain at the same time.

Such things well … not fun … not, well … anything.

It seems we were even given the warning so that we could come up with a much better drama, more fun for all for every place in consciousness throughout the Universe. For the Universe has already experienced such a bummer of a symphony, which is now just a red planet.…

It was much more fun, filled with life, creative divine noises, and manic whacky Chaplinesque movements, sounds, color, laughter, laughter, laughter. Not fun that one.[2]

Why not a hero's tale; no solitary hero, but billions and billions of heroes. Showing the Universe the story of the impossibly death-defying grasping at life, even as being thrown over the cliff. The solidarity in flesh, as united as in divine state, grasping single-handedly a bit of root protruding from the very edge above the abyss. And with mighty, united, happy, joyous, then singing, mighty and strong, pulling up, scraping knees, chins, shins, no matter, such incredible unity of peoples around the Globe as hasn't been seen since the time before that Tower, that time called Babel. That was a time when flesh decided to really stray from remembering and to really become solitary and alone, creating the darkness, which the light is so much sweeter by. Creating the horrible endless times of struggling, of violence, of ego over ego, with no one hearing, no one listening. But every one simply babbeling out THEIR world, *their* sounds, "The song must be like this!" "It is *my* song." "I am divine, who the hell are you to sing while I'm composing my next chorus!?"

And so it began, with the blissful knowledge of Unity with All That Is turning psychotically into

I AM the Unity, I am all that is. I am hardly experiencing the flows of consciousness that you are. For I AM the only consciousness. How could you be? You don't look like me; yet I am conscious and I am the Decider. So since I look like this and I act, and you look different, as different as I look compared to a pile of rubble, so you must not feel. You must be props for me to use.

And yet you jabber on, even as I am thinking, ever more, always thinking. I can't stop this thinking; I don't remember the world too well. That must be the price of being the only real living feeling existing thing here.

So it went. I don't know why. But then there is that thing about it all being about greater wisdom.

And perhaps, I think this a better story than a one-second sounding of the Universe in Pain…. For nowhere in that Universe would there be a being saying,

Now that was one great species! Really so godlike. Incredible. They lasted for one nanosecond and then simply slammed their entire species — even taking with them every other of the millions of different kinds of beings that Consciousness was tripping around with, in checking out.

No. I don't see our ending that way as being any more entertaining or enlightening than the shortest of all short stories about a man who walked across a busy freeway. Cleverly he avoided every car. He got increasingly adept and nimble. In his happiness he jumped to safety and stabbed himself to death with a knife. I told you, pretty dumb story.

I'd rather see people becoming the best humans that have ever lived on this planet at one time. And working together, not knowing even if they would make it, but knowing that the laughter of children depended on it. That laughter of children would be never again. And, in fact, who can say that it ever existed really?

There's Hope in That Never Before Has There Been Such a Worldwide Jonesing for Authenticity

Why Not Create a Story Together That Would Thrill God Herself?

So, if you feel like I do. If you would rather write, together with seven billion others, a story that will thrill God Herself, won't we be thrilled and never forget: How we took the best they had. They misinformed, spent untold huge amounts on those whose souls could be bought. And many there were, to deny, to repress, even when the rest of the world was waking up and looking to us for leadership.

America ... Earth Criminal

And America did not merely back off and, inexplicably, turn to throw back at the world a big ol' middle finger salute, grimacing, then turn and walk away. America, the wealthiest country in the world at that time.... Well at least its rich elite made it so, for its standard of living was getting lower by the year since the institution of the new slogan of democracy which was redefined in the early 1980s as, "of the people, by the people, to benefit the rich." America left the rest of the world to suffer and meet and discuss.

And all the time the world knew that they were like employees having a meeting without the boss showing up.... Nope, more like they were like the citizens who lived in a beautiful lake area, which had once been a pristine lake. But now the lake was dead, there were no fish living, lots of gooey seaweed though.

And sure they all contributed something to polluting that lake they did. But what was going to be done having meetings that had no representatives of the lumber milling company that sat on a good stretch of lakeside frontage and mindlessly had been spewing the most god-awful chemicals in the lake? It was going to be sickening the citizens soon. But this lumber operation also confused any deliberations that might have been fruitful by its habit of tossing around such huge gobs of money at selected groups of citizens.

So that's us, the fat bastards.

Apocalypse Is Real

I put whatever energy I can towards educating people about the dangers leading to apocalypse.

I am trying to help folks to understand they are not really believing apocalypse because it is too huge to comprehend. I try to get people to see that though they do not want to entertain the thought of apocalypse, it is real. Apocalypse is as real as your child suddenly lurching out of your hand to rush into the street just as a car is speeding there and getting killed.

Join with me or not as you will. I mention my efforts only to indicate the efforts of one person who has been awakened to this horrifying vision. Keep in mind there are others doing far more than me, for a longer time, and at greater risk.

Volunteers working with Greenpeace, Earth First, and similar organizations place their bodies directly in front of the attackers in a manner just like those prodemocracy activists living under dictatorial and totalitarian regimes who, Ghandi-style, stand in front of tanks and place their bodies before onslaughts of anti-aircraft weaponry (as happened not long ago in Libya).

There are others whose work also deserves more attention than mine, and in other places they are and will continue to be mentioned. But for purposes here, you get the point: No one can know how great are the forces of light arrayed against those of darkness on this issue, for the moneyed interests do not find it at all helpful to their side to allow the media to broadcast or highlight these efforts.

Rather, the media will exaggerate the activities and viewpoint of the opposition to these efforts, those that support the continued march toward Doomsday on whose road they collect heavy tolls from people to make up the obscenely exorbitant and evil profits they receive. They blow up the activities, viewpoints, and (mis)information in the exact same manner as in recent years they have, for example, amplified attention of, even promoted, Tea Party rallies attended by, mostly paid, hundreds while ignoring true grass roots action, as in Wisconsin, where a rally of two hundred thousand barely was mentioned. This is perhaps the meaning of the saying, "The revolution will not be televised."

In this obscurity of our efforts and its results lies our hope. For we simply will not know until later, maybe not even until an "afterward," assuming there is one, just how great are the efforts of the unheralded numbers involved in this undertaking.

Worldwide Craving for Authenticity

So, no, I am hardly the only one saying this. Quite to the contrary, there are lots of people now, more than ever before, who are fed up with being coddled from the truth and manipulated by lies and misinformation. Having been water boarded so many gallons of lies over Bush's eight years, they are showing the starvation they've been feeling for truth. Folks are painfully jonesing for something authentic in a number of ways.

Most spectacularly, Americans showed their craving for authenticity in the overwhelming 2008 turnout for Obama. At the time, Obama, over everyone else, was someone radiating realism, accountability, and authenticity.

Tea Party Ducklings

More recently we see this desperation pushing people to the Tea Party. Though sadly lacking in facts, fed misinformation by moneyed groups, manipulated, and directed to action by forces arrayed against their interests, Tea Party folks are newly birthed into politics following a burning knowing that something is terribly wrong and that they are being lied to. Like newly hatched ducklings, they are bonded to their corporate Mommies, who they follow blindly, fighting against those who would help them. On the other side, we see this eruption of truth-valuing in that, despite Tea Party's misguided actions, the polls show that Republicans, the party of organized deception in allegiance to interests of a global clique of "filthy rich," are seen to be more like fools than as credible opponents.[3]

What Would the Planetmates Say ... and Would You Respond You Are NOT "Stupid Ape"?

Still, facing the facts of the likely End of All Time, Doomsday, or Apocalypse — however you choose to phrase it — is not in anyone's hardwired capacities to handle. We are like ants suddenly confronted by a huge lumberjack's boot about to come smashing down on their meticulously created universe of AntHill. I doubt they, let alone we, have ever been programmed for such contingencies.

But humans are supposed to have the capacity to reason, to go beyond pure instinct, and to be able to prepare for the totally unprecedented. So far, our much-vaunted rationality is seeming like a pretty convenient rationalization to enable us to kill without conscience, for any reason we choose, the other species on this planet. How would our planetmates see it? Perhaps something like:

Humans Adopt Superiority Over All, Basing It On Their Inability to Keep Their Psychotic Minds from ever Stopping the Onslaught of Mental Verbiage. [Planetmate Views. Nowtime. Everyplace, Earth.]

Humans have created a bizarre separate and solitary view, which keeps them from seeing Reality, let alone God, who is directly before them. But they are committed to this psychosis of generating such a mental screen of words, which they mistake for actual reality.

Living In their self-imposed tortuous hell of verbal-mental realities, having nothing to do with reality, they neither see God, nor us planetmates, nor do they really hear each other. For humans pretend to listen but are really thinking of what they are going to say when it is their turn. So humans come away from conversations having only heard themselves. And now, their delusion is having them kill themselves all off; and they are not even all that concerned.

Unfortunately, they are taking ALL the rest of us, planetmates, indeed everything alive on this planet, down with them. Many of our fellow planetmates, in light of this, are questioning our compassion for their sorry half-born asses and our tolerance over the past twenty-five millennia.

You don't believe our planetmates? Natch. Didn't expect you to — sprung on you like that. But if what the planetmates say just for a moment pisses you off enough to say "NO, We are not stupid ape! We are rational!" Then you cannot be consistent without using some of that, ahem, ahem, so-called "reason." For before you can say NO to Apocalypse you have to let yourself KNOW Apocalypse. Now, how many of you have the cajonies or ovaries for that?!

David Bowie sang, "We could be heroes ... just for one day." Wow, that just occurred to me. It also occurred to me that being heroes just for one day never made any sense to me until just about, oh, like two seconds ago.

Well, I'm no hero. I just fucking care. Sorry if caring offends people so much they have to put down feeling people by saying "kumbaya moment." Sorry if caring offends so much they have to put down people who have hearts by saying "bleeding hearts." Or even when we have a President who sheds a tear and says in all sincerity, "I feel your pain," the cynical have to rake him over the coals for it and put it down in the history books as a calculated, planned, political move.

I'm sorry for people like that who have no felt connection with others. Such kitty-drowners and butterfly-mashers have no hearts and so do not understand those of us who do.

Before I took my personal journey inward and opened up to my feelings and eventually to the love that lie deep inside, I was more of a mental machine than a man.

Now, I am happy to be flesh and blood and feeling and organic —

I cry, fart, burp, laugh uproariously sometimes, actually, rolling on the floor. I see, hear, and notice people and think they are just fascinating. I can't imagine life back in the world of the machine-minded, bragging how they can multi-task, so they can fuck up more things at the same time. But never can such automatons focus on one thing at a time and completely take it in, in all its complexities.

But this isn't about the ones who will never hear me. It is about those who are just as much flesh and blood as I. You are the ones who will understand that I do this because, I just, well, really love.

I've got a young goddaughter; she reminds me what being straight and honest is. She also reminds me what love is, and how tender is the simple appreciation of one being for another. In my mind, my goddaughter is beautiful inside and out and talented and sensitive. She is God's work of art. I don't think there is a parent alive who doesn't know those kinds of feelings.

So, I don't know about other people, but with her in mind, among many others that I love, I find it hard to simply ignore the things that the scientists are saying are happening on this planet. Perhaps the most horrible for me to comprehend is the predicted massive extinction that is underway and is expected to reach a fifty percent die-off (forever, folks) of species on this planet in twenty to fifty years. You thought the bees disappearing was news!? Only if you can understand it as the canary in the coal mine.

If We Must, Without the Support of the Media, Rise to the Biggest Challenge of All, Would We Not Be Better to Face It?

We Got Too Many Species Anyway … And Other Stupid Denial Tricks Against Ecocide

A fifty percent extinction of life-forms on this planet within a few decades, many of which have been around for millions, even billions of years. And, are you thinking, hell, we got way too many species anyway? I know, dumb! But someone actually said that to me during the Q & A after a presentation I gave on this. And many in the audience seemed to think she had a point!![4]

Well, the planet is an ecosystem; it is like one giant life form. And it was once really healthy, perfectly balanced, like I said, a wonderful creation of God. It was an exquisite creation, reminding us that God is well, really, I mean, really, really, good!

Nope, not being facetious; just making my point in response to the general idea out there about God. That is, this insane prevailing notion that God is Infinite Goodness and Mercy beyond all human understanding, yet this Good God would create a hell where all but a lucky few would live, without being able to die, in hideous unbearable agony forever. Christ! I just heard myself realize that and if I were a kid I would've pooped my pants!

Ok, finishing up here. If you care about what's going on and think we should wake up, naturally you're discouraged at how little consciousness there is about an environmental collapse that has already begun. But there is hope at least in certain things. I've mentioned the craving for the real and the true. This powerful urge has toppled Bush, birthed an awkward tea-party movement, and shown the light on right-wing idiocy in America.

Around the world this explosive force manifests along with its correlates, the needs to express and share this truth in free speech and to have human rights to not be punished for that, as well as to have power for one's truth to effect one's life and circumstances, so there is the need for democracy. So it has fueled freedom and independence movements in nearly every country on Earth. In the last year alone, we have seen massive outpourings for human rights and justice in Turkey, Brazil, Romania, and Egypt — where only months ago the largest demonstrations in history were going on. In the Mideast and North Africa we see dictators being confronted and overthrown, and in China and similar totalitarian systems we see people risking and sacrificing their lives rather than be living beneath a cover of lies, behind a matrix of the contrived. Perhaps the most powerful way of all, this force is flowering worldwide as an Occupy movement, encouraging everyone to Occupy Earth, among many other things.

As to where this effort will lead.... Well, the hopeful question is: Who knows how many others are also feeling like we don't have a second to lose, and it might already be too late? Who knows what kind of actions might be needed to be done, and what kind of word might need to get out, or whatever?

If You Knew What I Knew, Would You Do Less?

Finally, looking over my efforts alone, one might even be thinking I am overdoing it. But consider that I believe what I'm saying: A trillion-alarm emergency, the lives of my loved ones at stake. Now, if you knew what I knew, would you do less?

But this isn't about me, I am only mentioning my work alongside the fact that I felt finally like I could speak out in this country only when Obama was sworn in as President. Who knows how many efforts are going on, how many kinds of things people are doing to stave off this Unthinkable Nightmare? Now, with Bush no longer in power, when finally we have the world and its efforts, however difficult they still will be, at least not being actively undermined by a Republican administration, we have a time where we have more hope that our efforts will succeed based upon the good will of the participants, without worrying excessively that the mighty U.S. will at some point either secretly or overtly throw the grandest of all monkey wrenches in to shatter the work of the good people of the world working heartily on the side of Life.

So, if you care, we might as well start making that network now. And I know there are others. But there can never be too many connections bringing together all of us who care.

Don't forget we're going up against a bunch who DON'T care, but who are, as they termed them, not me! "Filthy Rich." And great power they have indeed for you know how many there are who are for sale and how cheaply souls are going for these days. But we have, if we choose it, the power of solidarity, truth, and — if we can awaken enough people — the power of great, great, grand numbers on a scale that also has never been possible before.

So, I urge everyone to remember that they are in the midst of a trillion-alarm fire. The emergency is upon us; unfortunately it is not being broadcast. But some of that is because it is too dire for the media to want to touch. So it is up to us.

We must remember that it has always been the common people of the world uniting in great numbers that have accomplished the things of greatest value to the world. If we must once again, and without the support even of the media, rise to the biggest challenge of all, then why would we not be the better ones to face it? For the elite have already shown that they care little for anything but their profits.

Whereas it is the common people of the world, taking their pleasure in their pride of work, and especially their families, who have put themselves always on the line. We need only remember that it is not for us, or even for all the innocent creatures of the world — though that would be huge motivation for many — but if only so that our children and grandchildren will not suffer, will get to live, and hopefully will be awarded at least the chance that other generations got for a full life, we must give our all.

I cannot believe that the masses of people in the world, were they ever to come to understand the true consequences — the life and death ones — for their immediate family — would not do everything including risking one's own life, for something so precious — the continuation of family … the laughter of children, the innocence of a babe, and above and beyond everything, the continuation of Love, sweet, sweet, ever growing and expanding Love, under the blessings and grace of The All that Is, whose substance is just that — Love.

CHAPTER 3

CONVERSATION ON THE EVE OF APOCALYPSE

AN ANATOMY, IN STORY FORM, OF THE MACHISMO ATTITUDE TOWARD OUR END

Facing Apocalypse, People Are Bccoming Zombies

People are becoming zombies in the face of their death, their own upcoming suffering, not to mention the death of all life on this planet. Do an internet search on *apocalypse* and note how little, if anything, is posted about the urgency or emergency of our current situation.

It comes across as a big party on a South Pacific Island in a hotel that cveryone there knows will not survive the incoming tsunami or killer hurricane. But in the meantime they're drinking themselves silly, drugging ... gonna party their way to the end. That is not a rational response to the end of all life.

Other responses on the apocalypse have machismo aspects to them. In fact, most sites about apocalypse have a macho message in common.

Macho, Macho Man

You are not going to believe it, but check it out: The theme ... now look deeply, if you're not used to picking up on people's motives off hand ... the theme goes something like this:

Well, folks, we're all gonna die. But big deal. I'm so fucking macho, I laugh at death! Here, let me prove it to you. Come here, death, right up to my face!

See, everybody. How I look directly into this face, this face of death! Now watch. Watch as I spit, spit directly into this face. Ptoo! (spits) See that? So who cares!? Not convinced? Then watch and I'll show you. See the face of death that I'm holding and facing? Watch as I laugh in its face, laugh directly in its face. HA! Hahahahahaha! See? Told you.

Doing it, Tron style

Well, that is the way it comes across: "Apocalypse? Let me show you how tough I am." Not, "What can we do about it, to stop it?"

So, dear listeners, are you able to make out the distress beneath such pronouncements? Granted, this bravado is worthless as to either reversing apocalypse or even showing some sort of inspired vision in which it can be made acceptable or noble if not avoidable. For those who do not see it yet, in this chapter I try a little fantasy dialogue to bring out what I think is going on, much of the time, and keeping us from acting rationally about this imminent emergency of all dire emergencies possible.

Witness me as I trip over in cyber-land to something I call Amalgamated Macho-Apocalypto-dot-com. I'm about to go over to the webmaster of that site, in imagination and, well, just run a question or two past him. Tune in and catch what ensues. It should be revealing. Hang on one second, while I fly myself over. See you there!

Spitter Dude

Ok, I'm here. And there he is with his death skull T-shirt on. I'm going to go over to him, just watch.

"Hey, yo dude! Deathface spitter and laugher!"

"You … You know me … ?"

"Hell yeah. You're in Google, you know. I understand you're surprised because, believe me, tagged with *apocalypse*, like you, well, let's just say I don't have to lock the doors either. But there's probably more interest in you than what I do."

"Really, more interest in me? I like that! What do you do then?"

"On my site I tell the truth: you know, tell them that it's very very bad and looks impossible unless people wake up on a massive scale and decide unequivocally to live. Stuff like that."

"Ha. Hahahahaaha."

"Ok, but just no spittin. I've seen your routine."

"No, no. Nothing of the sort. No, really, I thought that kind of stuff died in the Sixties with all the 'kumbaya' and 'we shall overcome' baloney."

Why's Everybody Hatin' on Kumbaya?

"Well, not that it'll make a difference on you, but yeah, I'm that old and have had many high moments of unity in among the angels of humans coming forth to reunite — what you refer to as *kumbaya*. And by the way, I like the song, I like the Lord, what's everybody pissed at? As for the other, we overcame. I've really dug being me because I've had the pleasure of being part of the things that made the world better; and I can't imagine a better high or feeling of fulfillment.

"But I'm not here to dispute with you. I'm an old fart who got to live in rich times and participate in them. You're a young, well, younger-than-me person, who was apparently born at around the time all the things my kind were working for were deemed a threat to the status quo. And so the powers-that-be created the misinformation, scapegoating, and slander of my generation. Then they delivered to generations following mine the machismo cynicism with its connotation that it was better to have that than feeling life. They seeded you with the idea that those who experienced life ... as opposed to those who accepted their prepackaged attitudes of cynicism and mean-spiritedness ... well, we were wusses, saps, effeminate, feminate, and all that.

"So, sorry, that my generation's threat to the moneyed powers was so scary to them that they reacted with the all-out effort to create a generation that would be the opposite of us, and so you were brainwashed and misinformed and lied to. So, so very sorry. I wish I could say, "my bad," but well it was "our good" that resulted in "their bad," and I don't want to be like them and continue to uphold their matrix of misinformation. So, anyway, sorry."

"Well, I shoulda set that to record for later. That was waaaay too much and too many twist and turns for me to follow. But you called yourself an old fart. That part I got. So since you've placed yourself below me, I guess I'm at ease with your being here, whatever it is."

Who Ya Talkin to, Dude?

"Well, your Dudeness, your Fearlessness Most Strong and Mighty, I have a few humble questions to ask of you," I say.

"Ok, old fart, go ahead."

"I see clearly that you're showing the world you don't fear death. But how is that going to help the world any. I mean if everyone felt like you ... let's say that was your aim ... well then we'd all go down, patting each other on the back on how it doesn't matter, but never to be heard of again!"

"Your point?" he says, irritated.

"Are you saying my site isn't offering anything to the world? So who the hell says a site has to be doing anything for anybody or anything? Let alone this world....

"This is *me*! I'm *expressing* me! What else is there to do?"

"Ok, thank you. That explains a lot. But something comes to me. May I?"

"Sure," says he.

"You say that, 'this is me.' Number one. Right?"

"Right." Annoyed again.

"Ok. Now, you know there are not a lot of people watching. But your intention is not to influence any people. Number two, right?"

"Yep, that's right."

"But you wouldn't be putting up a website if you didn't want somebody to know who you are. I mean, you could say it in the mirror, or in your bedroom. You wouldn't be making it available unless there's somebody, persons, that you hope would hear you. Would that not be number three, right?"

"Well, you old farts really are big on this self-analytical crap, aren't you? Well, I ain't no pussy, but I am man enough to say that I couldn't escape the logic that ... yeah, I am, inside, wanting to share, and share myself to some, to some ... well, I guess, I just wouldn't mind if, uh, really by accident of course, some people, who never got to know me this way, might see me and understand ... well, uh...."

Let's Play a Mind Game.

"Oh, *understand*. Nothing wrong with that. But, uh, how 'bout you indulge an old fart and just try out something that I think will be a real gas for you, er, perhaps I should say, *phat*, er, uh ... . Look, you can trust me to take the time to play a little, let's say, mind-game. It's lots of fun."

"Haha. Suure, ok. You crack me up, ya old fart. Gonna be a real gas. Ya can bet your damn asscrack that you'd lost me for sure until you'd made real quick to explain that one, heh heh."

So, I say, "Yep, that's a little mind-game prank that was played on me. Well, anyway, uh ... . Well, uh, I just want you to allow yourself to open your mind to the greater intentions — intentions you have for doing this, the *greater* visions. Now, don't think just yet, you'll only try to make things up. This is easier than that."

"*Ok.*"

"Ok, now. You say that ... being honest and only rational after all ... that of *course* you wouldn't be doing this expression of yourself *on the internet* if you didn't have some desire to share or show this part of you with somebody or somebodies in the world ... right? So far?"

"Yeah, get on with it, I've already said that."

"Ok, fine. Now, here's the fun part. I want you to have that desire … to have it *clearer* … the clearer you can make it, y'know, the more likely it will happen. So let me help you a little here. Now just clooose your eyes. No, no, don't look that way at me, nothing fishy going on…. You just ain't going to be able to see your desires with all the distractions that the sights around us present. Give it a chance. Believe me, I'm not trying to lay any trip on you…."

"Ok, that's better.

Who's Your Real Audience?

"Now. On the internet, we never see our audience. But we all imagine and wonder who they might be and what kind of people they are. Don't you, too?"

"Yeah, sure."

"Well, we're gonna try do something like that. Instead of an internet with no audience, well, imagine you're in an auditorium. It can still be an internet to you … and you're making the same points … and you're really getting into it, like: *I SPIT* (ptoo!) in the face of death … and *I LAUGH* uproariously in the face of death.

"How's it goin?"

"Yeah, I'm doing it, really into it … like it!"

"Ok. How does it make you feel?"

"Strong, *fucking* strong, *damn* fucking strong."

"Greeeat. You're feeling strong, real fucking strong. Feel as fucking strong as you can!"

"Great, yeah, all right, I'm so fucking strong, ain't no mother-fucking dudes as strong as me ... I spit, I laugh...."

"Very, very wonderful. Enjoy, enjoy that!... Now ... add one more thing.... One *more* thing, make it even better.... Remember, you're in an auditorium, and *here* you can see your audience. Stay with that 'spittin at death' strength. You're strong!... Now, containing all that strength ... all that *bigger* than death power ... cast your eyes down below you to the people in the audience ... you're at your peak! ... the people that you really wanted to show. You're strong, you're powerful, more powerful than death, right?"

"Fucking right, I am."

"Ok, now. *Show* them, and *tell* me who they are ... one by one ... look around ... slowly ... who do you really ... *really* want to show who you really are ... who couldn't see this before in you ... but now, they wouldn't be able to miss it? Take your time...."

"No need to take time! Ha! I'm fucking really strong now. And there's my *bitch* ex-girlfriend. Ha! Now, she doesn't seem so high and mighty. She looks scared now. Ha! She left me. Took off with some guy who did some kind of daredevil or motorcycle stunts. Sorta like saying to me, that, I wouldn't be there for her.... Well, she didn't get it then, but she's gettin' it now ... how much braver it is to stare down death than to face some motorcycle risks. Ha! Yeah, I'm gettin' it. This *is* fun. You're an old fart, but you got some tricks ... good tricks...."

"Ok, now," I say. "Look around, who else?"

"Well, there's several other girlfriends. Wow! How great to see the look on their faces now." (chuckling) "And there's my two older brothers. I really wanted to be like them, and ... hang out with them. But they made it like I wasn't big or tough enough. Boy, am I showing them now. How fucking glorious. Even they are scared; they are tooo chickenshit to do what I'm doing. Ha! I'm showing them ... heh heh heh....."

Those Damn 'Ghostly' Others

"Keep looking," I say.

"Ok, well, there's … there…. No. No … what the fuck, what the fuck's he here for?"

"Who's that?" I say.

"Why my dad … and my mother too. My dad always made me feel like I was weak just 'cause I was a kid. Why wouldn't I be weaker than a grown man!? That *bastard* never gave me credit for having the strength I've got. Yet how strong is he? Just because he can put down my mom and … who would never fight back…."

I say, "Look into his face. Did you show him? Does he finally see?"

"Not sure…. He's, he's kinda lookin' *down*…."

"Look more closely. Zoom in."

"OK…. Oh my god, that mother-fucking bastard, that prick!"

"What's going on?"

"Well, he's even angrier now. He's thinkin': 'What kinda pussy son he's got who's play-actin' all over the internet about how tough he is … but *that's* not bein' tough,' he's thinkin'…. Why that fuck! He never did understand *any*thing I did, he put down *every*thing I did. I *tried*, but no matter. I could *never* be man enough … in *his* eyes…."

I say, "That's rough, dude, rough. That'd be hard for anyone to live through…."

"Yeah." Beginning to choke up. "Yeah…" he says … he's sobbing now.

"That *mother*.... All those years I had to live with that *fuck!* ... hope and try and not getting *any*thing back ... my God! ... except ... *scorn! Gaaa! Scorn!* Scorn and *Hate!* It's *you* who's face I spit in, *you*'re the fuckin' death, I hate you!... I'm bigger than you. I survive you. I laugh! Ooooh...."

And Spitter Dude broke off crying.

You're never gonna win, pal, give it up already.

Well. I did what I could for him...and stayed with him and hung out with him for a while.... Really not a bad guy at all. He seemed to really get it, too, that he didn't *need* to do things to prove to his dad anymore, because he could clearly see there was no extreme he could ever go *to* or ever go *through* that would make a dent in his father's attitude of despising him.

I explained that while it is hard to accept that his father really did despise him, that he will find it easier than most, because he at least *knew* it ... and didn't try to pretend it wasn't true. But that he just hadn't gotten it out of his craw that even in some imaginary way he could get *some*thing that he just wasn't meant to get in this life. And I explained that, that is the way with all of us. There's always something that's not part of the perfect family portrait, or there's some elephant in the room.

I explained that, while he didn't have to prove anything anymore to his father that, while he was doing it, it led him to learn a lot about the internet and such, and he could apply that to something new.

So when I was leaving, he said something. It gave me a happy thought. He said:

"You know. Now I don't *need* to show anybody anything. What a waste of time that was."

What to Do, When You Don't *Have* to Do

And he continued, "It occurs to me, then … 'What the hell to do'? Then it occurs to me, 'Well, if you got nothing to prove, and you really don't *want* the world to end, actually.' In fact, it is pretty scary.

"And I'm thinkin' of all the innocents … like my mom … being put down by big scary men whose only strength lies in putting down little kids, and their wives … so they can feel strong. Hmm….

"So I think, 'No, there's no changing my dad.'

"But the next thing I have is … 'While my mother isn't here anymore, there's lots of helpless innocents out there, like her, who aren't being helped … about what's coming down.' They're even being prevented from knowing, by other chickenshit men like my dad, who are only out for themselves and it doesn't matter who they hurt … s'long as they get their *profits*.

How DARE They?

"So, I'm thinkin' this, and I'm real surprised because I feel myself breathing deeper. And I feel some anger coming, like, 'How DARE they?!'

"And then some strong feelings of manliness … my heart crying out … like to my mother. Even choking up a little, thinkin' like, 'I'll take care of you, young mother, little sister, little brother, little baby child. I'm bigger, I'm stronger. I'll protect you from harm' … like no one protected me. And now I know how *horrible* that was. And, how I could do nothing to … and how I would do *any*thing to stop that from happening to others. I really would. And I got all psyched! Y'know?

Guaranteed to Bring Out the Best in You

"I'm sorry for putting you down about wanting to help the world. Cause I see that's the best place to put your strength and to be a real man.... Y'know? To have a just cause ... put all your strength into it ... whether you win or not. Just to be on the right side! And in the meantime to stand between any hardship and those innocents ... and to comfort their sorry hearts. It seems like there's no other worthy thing to do."

Well, I expressed how that was *really* wonderful. And I said ... to confirm for him ... I said how this is the biggest struggle this planet has ever faced.

And, he's right: It is the worthiest effort that one can imagine. And guaranteed to bring out the best in us ... and to make us better ... as well as the worst in us ... which we can at least know and struggle with to keep those things from undermining the good in us.

Freed From a Prison

Well, after that we talked about how we individually and together could do things in the future, and ... . It gladdened my heart to see him freed from the prison of striving forever for a love that would never be and ... to be learning, already, that true love is in giving.

That true love is in giving.

Finding love, in giving love

No doubt, if he continues like this, he'll soon learn that in giving love, he finds more love than his heart can contain, coming his way, without his expecting, asking, or even seeing it coming. I wouldn't be surprised if he comes over to my site to contribute, share, and even join in solidarity.

Could Be *Real* Men, Instead of Performers for Phantom Puppeteers

Well, that's one take on why people are not reacting to the seriousness of the end of all life on this planet. I think it's a rather pervasive one. And I'm sure there are others. And I just wish it would be that easy to turn these people around to see how they could be *real* men, how they could be *real* heroes, how they could be really strong. Instead of performing for some "ghostly" others … who aren't there, and … who aren't going to be impressed anyway.

Take my word for it or not. That's the way I see it.

Other Takes on This

Other irrational responses and reactions to the end of all time are discussed in the next two chapters, "Death Wish — Zombie Apocalypse and Sympathy for the Bedeviled," and "Thanatos Walking and the Only Question."

CHAPTER 4

DEATH WISH — ZOMBIE APOCALYPSE AND SYMPATHY FOR THE BEDEVILED

Zombie Apocalypse

People put up fronts of false bravado to defend against their apocalyptic fears, but they also deaden themselves to the facts. We have climate deniers now, who are going around saying we have no problem with global warming. No, they say, that is all a story by some bad folks who just want to control us. To which I think, seriously, how convenient. Is it not obvious they are engaging in desperate wish fulfillment?

Also, look around you in the cities or on the internet. The people you see have no concern, let alone awareness, of their dire predicament ... no urgency or apocalypse emergency. It is the veritable *zombie apocalypse* before us. It is no wonder that folks are enamored of this revolting image of walking dead people everywhere, which we see on the silver screen and pervades our current cultural consciousness.

Indeed, what we see surrounding us in the numbed and deadened responses to our apocalypse emergency is the most disturbing of any evidence I have seen supporting what Sigmund Freud called *Thanatos,* that is to say, the Will to Die.[1]

EnRaptured Reaction

But false bravado and zombification are the most insane responses to our situation with one glaring exception: That is, what we hear as being a euphoric longing for the end of it all in evangelical groups who think of it as *the Rapture* — a kind of being freed from what is seen as an onerous Earth existence and the reward of the true life one thinks one deserves of ease, love, and happiness in heaven.

Now, is that not the most extreme form of reaction formation you have ever heard? These folks have developed an elaborate, comforting fantasy to escape the facts of their lives.

These "enraptured" people are the same ones who admit /claim they were the good little God- (parent-) fearing children who slavishly fawned upon the unreal wishes of their authoritarian parents — parents who themselves were real religious nutjob psychotics whose lived world was an imaginary one of hellishness and a stern bearded father god who makes you say, even think, that he is loving — despite being the most horrendously mean and more-than-murderous mythical figure ever concocted.[2]

Gotta Love 'im, He's the … Monster!

For this father "god" will not just punish by ending one's life but will punish you in what has to be the most extreme kind of punishment ever to be imagined — being forced to live forever but every moment of it being in extreme pain and suffering.

And these folks have to somehow twist their brains into thinking this "god," this monster, is actually loving rather than the obvious.

The parents bought that horrific view of the ultimate reality of it all; then their kids slavishly followed them in this insanity. Is it any wonder then that their wish is to be dead!?[3]

Reaction Formation ... Leave It to Humans!

So the reaction formation is that of creating the kind of life where, unlike their own childhood, they would be loved, cherished, seen, made to feel special, and so on. Most of all to be freed from the fear of punishment of the most extreme form imaginable. Leave it to humans to be so cut off from the reality of a loving God as to wish to be dead instead. For they have managed, with their imagination running loose and totally without even one lifeline to anything loving or nice — either in their own life's experiences or in the mythology of reality they have been forced to accept — to come up with the most unimaginably horrible view of their lives, and its prospects.

But they'll give you "breathing holes"!

One last reversal of reality, what Freud called *reaction formation,* is that — getting "breathing holes" this way, "thinking they are happy" — they call themselves "saved" and think it is their duty to go out and "save" everyone else in the world.[4]

For, in the view of *enraptured* folks, others are suffering and miserable. Interestingly, this is similar to the way they view the "animal" world — our planetmates — and the World of Nature in general.[5]

Also, others needing to be "saved" like them insinuates that their happiness — the state of being of the "enraptured" — is eminently superior to the experienced lives of all others.

The media enables these psychotics.

Now, isn't it about time we stopped giving in to their pestering and stopped adding media credibility to their huge denial systems? For our sakes, yes, but for them as well. For this media credibility just aids them in their sickness, and their continued misery.

At any rate, we have here reaction formation and then reinforcement of it by the media.[6]

En-Raptured Proselytists' Apocalyptic Death Wish

So these sad proselytists know deep inside how miserable they are. But they find a way to stave off the realization of that reality and of its horrible roots in their suffering in childhood, through denying their unhappiness. They take up arms against their misery and engage in an endless battle trying desperately to believe ... and unfortunately for us, assert ... that the opposite is true: That is, that their experience is happy.

Sad Proselytists

This sad insanity they impose on all and everyone. Of the actual pathetic nature of their lives they know intuitively but without letting themselves think it. That is not unlike the way they handle any of the other uncomfortable truths and "inconvenient" facts of their lives, by the way.

Desperate Affirmations

They also know in their muscles that saying the lie out, and loudly, can help in reinforcing their precious untruths. For these dear fabrications, when heard coming from the outside — even if it is simply one's own voice that one is hearing echoed back — have greater weight and credibility to them. When experienced existing in the outside world, they can be felt to be more real than when heard just in one's own private thoughts alone.[7]

This is another reason they need to enlist other people, and have the media echo it: It adds to the reality of these lies ... the Big Lie repeated becomes more true ... and boosts their defense against, and attacks on, the truth of their reality which asserts itself over and over — "truth will out" — during their life and increasingly more as they get older. This also explains their behavior's increasing rigidity with time, and its downright obdurate nature when these folks become curmudgeons, so typical of the elderly.

If YOU accept that I'm better off than you, then I must be!

But simply proclaiming their blessed savedness out loud is not enough to be truly convincing over against the unhappiness that they actually feel every moment. So the big guns are brought out: Not only must they proclaim their happiness; they can PROVE it. This leads to their fantasy of engaging with the rest of the world in convincing all others that they are indeed less happy than they think they are and that that they need and want the "saving" the "enraptured" ones are offering.

The underlying rationale goes like this: If you could convince others in the world that you were happier than they are to the point where those others would all want to give up their lives and have your life instead, well, then that PROVES you are happy, or at least that what you have is the happiest existence possible. You are the "winner" in life, essentially.

For if your reality wasn't the better one, no one would choose it over their own ... no one would decide to try to be like you rather than to be like themselves. Conversely, other people choosing to try to become like you, to accept your beliefs ... to be "saved" ... proves that your reality is the superior one (One Way!!). To such lengths do people go to deny their sad, unfortunate lives.

Inner lepers

If one could not see the tragedy of it for a moment, one would have quite a belly laugh, at their sake: Just this vision of inner lepers, convincing themselves that they are divinely gifted healers instead, going out to convince as many healthy people as possible that it is they who have leprosy and that they (the actual inner lepers proclaiming themselves spiritual healers) can cure them (of this disease that they don't have) by the laying on of hands ... or magical words repeated endlessly (endlessly ... endlessly ... endlessly....) and as loudly as possible.

Sympathy for the Bedeviled

However, you simply have to take a look at the lives described above and imagine those multitudes and the incredible pain, utter lovelessness, utterly miserable and confused minds they carry as adults.

Then think beyond them to the many-fold more of the masses who have similar but lesser versions of lives and experiences as the "enraptured."

Add to that the incredible power of fear ... not only fear; but fear that has, well, demonically, been projected into the biggest expanse existing in the universe — that of the imagination and that of the knowledge of the Unknown, combined.

A Mind That's Squirming Like a Toad

If you can get a sense of that fear, even a small part, you will realize the utter terror that awakens them, that is there in the middle of the night as they approach consciousness, and which, like a squirming frog, inhabits, nay, becomes the daytime brain and thoughts of these people, and motivates them to do ANYTHING, anything at all, that might promise a snippet of relief from what is the reality they condemn others to.

You will see that they believe in hell because they in fact live lives that are the closest things in existence to actual hells. This is made that much worse, indeed, multiplied many times over, by the idea implanted with it, which is that to acknowledge that truth will actually result in the imagined hell becoming reality ... and that the only way they can save themselves from that hell is to, somehow, not be aware of their own reality as it is. So they must struggle mightily to not know what they indeed do know.

Now, try that burden on for size. And just be glad that you are not them. They exist within that nightmare reality; they see it portrayed before them. They have not even the respite, like watching a horror movie, of ever walking out of the theater and thinking, "Well, I'm glad that was only a movie."

But the rest of us must confront their horrible realities as well. Sorry, you are not spared them. And you dare not take comfort in looking away from them either. For to deny that this is what they are doing is the same as denying the events of history that have resulted from these kinds of horrible existences: all the wars, killings, tortures, holocausts, purges, genocides, pogroms.

It is no coincidence that these sorry sorts are attracted to fantasies of denial, such as denying climate change, denying the Holocaust, denying the atrocities committed by religions or their own governments. In striving to be shiny, happy people they create inner hells and outer monsters. Not only hell do they create, but all the hellacious things on earth are the offspring of these lives. This includes the creation now of the ultimate evil that can be committed while in flesh — the killing of the planet and of all life on it.

Thanatos Walking Your Way

For a final take on insane or irrational reactions to the end of time and of all life on this planet, another example of the Will to Die, continue to the next chapter, "Thanatos Walking and the Only Question."

CHAPTER 5

THANATOS WALKING AND THE ONLY QUESTION

APOCALYPSE IS HOW AN OVER-ACHIEVING SPECIES LIKE OURS DOES ITS WILL TO DEATH

Freud showed we had a will to die ... so — Will we survive? Will we wake up from global apathy to save our planet? Will we resist cowardly denial or die out like the dinosaurs?

Will We Survive?

This chapter discusses an age-old question which has currently become of immense, literally vital, importance: Will our species survive or die out like the dinosaurs? is the most crucial issue of our time. It is related to the fundamental fact of our existence for it is about the struggle between the forces of Life and those of Death. The consequences as to the winner of that inner struggle have to do with no less than the continued survival of life on this planet or total planetary collapse.

Eros Versus Thanatos

In the struggle between the current powers of life and death, it is helpful to remember Freud's paradigm-shifting observations about the human psyche on Eros and Thanatos. Freud showed how all human lives are drawn out against the background of each person's inner struggle between the opposing forces of life and death ... Eros and Thanatos. Specifically, for our purposes here, Freud advanced an understanding that made his insights paradigm-shifting, specifically, that each of us carry within us a Will to Die, which he referred to as *Thanatos*.

"Sometimes the Lights Are Shining on Me."

Freud established that we act out a will to live and to be in the sun and to have fun and to love and to like goodness and health and truth.

"Other Times I Can Barely See."

Freud also saw that we have at other times an opposite feeling that causes us to want to live in the dark; to not be around people; to shy away from life and the light and being seen and recognized and even to wanting to be lonely. This feeling causes us to not care about fun, to hate and be angry, indeed to hate everyone and even to want to lash out at them for no reason other than what might be self-labeled as spite. It makes us jealous of those who find happiness or pleasure in their lives and impels us to lash out at them and make them suffer the way we, on the inside, know that we do. Because of this self-defeating tendency we irrationally beat up on our own bodies as well and abuse them with all kinds of substances and behaviors.

Thanatos is why there are always Republicans or something like them — Pharisees, Inquisitors ...

And times in which they hold sway — stifling, life- and creativity-averse, stagnant and little changing times: the Middle Ages, for example. ...

This downward pull makes us want to hate goodness, calling things "kumbaya moments." This part of our nature causes us to be jealous of others who are more giving and to hate them for that, to call people "goody two-shoes" or say something is "schmaltzy," or to be saying that all that good stuff is just "drama." It has us putting out terms like "bleeding heart" liberals. It causes us to not care about the truth, but rather to say things instead to hurt, get revenge, to get back at. Or it has us say untruths to get advantage, to disable our competitors, to hide from the evils we commit which enslave us further in the hiding of them, and so much more.

Struggle Will Out

But Freud took it beyond our inner struggles and talked about how the events of the world, the actions and movements of history, and the dramas of all the ages are in fact the products of this inner struggle.

At this very moment, our lesser selves are taking us on a path that leads inevitably, one way or another, to total species extinction. But not just that, being the "overachieving" species we are, we are bringing total life extinction to this planet and possibly even planetary annihilation — the death of virtually all life on this Earth.

Well, Ain't We Special?

Freud pointed out we have a Will to Live, too — nothing earth-shattering there. In fact, so far he is stating nothing more than the common-sensical beliefs of the masses. Indeed, it is the universally held mainstream near-definition of humans ... one of those "obvious truths" about us we like to bless ourselves with. Freud's first point, taken by itself, encapsulates the clichéd view of What We Are — that what distinguishes our species above all others revolves around a superior Will to Life.

While common-sensical that our Will to Life is part of a species superiority of ours, it is wrong ... going too far. For would anyone say that other species don't also have an incredible Will To Live?

Not So Much

But this hyperbole or over-reaching in stating humans are unique in the degree of their Will to Life reinforces my point about Freud's ideas being zeitgeist-shattering. For in this common, frequent, pervasive even universal, and nauseatingly repeated promulgation of supposedly the obvious, by any and all who speak before an audience — large or small, from a principal speaking in front of a gathering of high schoolers or a preacher before his gathering of church-goers to the TV media pundit before a world-wide audience, and even to a US President's audience of even greater global reach — it is shown that our special Will to Life is not as true as is assumed. For if we had such a superior drive in us, would it need to be constantly reinforced and upheld, as if against some attack, or attacker? And if so, what is the feared attack or attacker?

And here we get a clue into Freud's discovery and its utter undermining of all that which is normally said regarding our humanness. For regarding our being special in our Will to Live, this kind of "protesting too much" and its flip side of repeating it *ad nauseum*, as Shakespeare obviously saw points to a hidden agenda. Truths do not have to be repeated endlessly, *mantram*-like, even ritualistically. For they are self-evident and need as much propping up as the belief that the sky appears to be the color blue to us — and you don't hear much about that, do you?

My Dogma Barks Out My Specialness

But the pervasive repetition of the supposed Truth of our species Will to Life — especially the blown-up version that has it being the thing that makes us human, different from other species, "superior" to other species (there's a clue), and even "special" (clue. Getting it?) — points to its being, not so much truth as dogma. And dogma *does* need to be endlessly repeated in that such things are exactly about things that are not obvious truths.

In fact, this repetition of an obvious truth points to its being *not* true. In the previous chapter I described how our "sad proselytists" have to say their untruths and unrealities out loud in order to buck up or reinforce their believability. So also human societies need to endlessly repeat, in order to reinforce against onslaughts of insight, *their* precious untruths.

But the reasons behind the promulgation of this supposed "obvious truth" go even beyond, since we are not dealing here with any conscious or acknowledged, let alone written and standardized, set of things not obvious. For indeed, in this sad repetition of our superior life-valuing, it is put out as being something not needing institutional backing, being simply true in its obviousness.

So what then? Well, this repetitive characterization of Us, as Humans, has all the indications of something that has an intention, however unconscious, that has a calculation, however desperate our desire to not see it, about it to achieve an effect on the audience — in this case — the masses of all humans.

Humans' Uniqueness Among Species? We Suck Up

What is that pathetically overlooked intention? Well, let us take a look at what that effect might be.

Anytime you place our species above all others (true or not), you

59

are making as much as anything else a play to butter up your audience of fellow humans and appeal to their vanity ... and thus, making them feel good, hoping that they will feel good, or, like you in return. In commonspeak, that's called "people-pleasing." In the vernacular, it's called "sucking up."

OK, so we've established that people in front of audiences nearly universally want to say things that will make their audience feel good towards them. No, not so fast. For that overlooks the fact that *somehow* ... and get this; for if the spoken thing were of the obvious truth category, then why would this follow ... that *somehow* all these people speaking out to others about the unique will to life they have know — somewhere inside them — that saying such a thing will, in fact, give people a good feeling. That's another clue.

More Socratic Dialoguing

And again, continuing this Socratic dialogue, well, wouldn't humans just, of course, feel good hearing about their being superior? Doesn't everyone feel good when told they are better and such? Well, now we're getting to where Freud took us. For he knew, as we all do if we simply think about it. The answer is "no, not necessarily or even usually."

Think about it. If the Beatles were to be told they were a good band, would that give them a good feeling? No. certainly not. For that was so true as to be overwhelming and almost scary in its near-universal belief. And we can suppose that to them having that kind of power and influence because of their talent — especially when you come out of nowhere, from humble, unassuming backgrounds — may have been distressing to think about and hardly something wanted from others. How could they not wonder about this power, its source, where it would lead, and all that? I don't think it happenchance that this success sent all of them into drug-taking — to both block it out as well as come to terms with it — into soul-searching of the spiritual and, especially John, of the therapeutic sort. Sometimes one does not want to be reminded of how "good" (and therefore powerful ... therefore *responsible*) one is; there's such a thing as feeling one is *scary good*.

Or take the obviously accomplished anybody, Pavarotti, say. Wanna tell Pavarotti he sings good? Don't think he'd feel a thing.

But, you say, that's because they hear that all the time.

Ok, granted that. But think about when it would have felt good to them. Look to your own experience and you realize that you feel good when people tell you things about yourself — especially when they state them as self-evident and obvious to all — about which you are not certain, about which you often or at least sometimes have doubts, and about which you are insecure! Look to your own life. Can anyone be flattered about the things they know to be without question? Can you be flattered about the color of your skin or hair, or about.... Well, not stated as a fact, you wouldn't. A person would be flattered only if they had some bad feeling, insecurity in that area, first; and second, if that quality of them is not usually noted though it be assumed by everyone to be a good, positive, or "superior" thing.

This pervasive, mutual stroking we do has a result which is of dire consequence currently: We scapegoat our planetmates because of this pathetically low self-esteem of ours and those who play on it. For we tell ourselves that we humans value life, that is, we have a stronger will to live, than any other living being on this planet. We call our lives "sacred."

While life may indeed be sacred, the idea usually put forth is that it is *only* our lives that are sacred. We are able to rationalize any atrocity or death inflicted on any other being as being justified if it adds to or enhances our lives even an iota.

What is part of that rationalization is that humans are *special* and *superior* in Nature in the degree of our Will to Life. We add to that spurious self-massage a narrative of Life making its way out of primeval ooze, rising up, lumbering across expanses of difficulty and effort, looming up larger and larger, until it makes its happy way to the haven of our elevated state of being. We say we are the pinnacle of evolution and the crown of creation. We stroke our egos with the balm of us being Life Itself, even, the reason for all those lesser experiments in animation. Out of a world of Nature which we deem characterized by casual and meaningless death, we lay claim to being the product of a transcendent Will to Life.

But rarely does the Siren call of ego line up with the song of Truth … in *any* instance. So we might question how deserving we are of the honors we heap upon ourselves in Earth's kingdom.

Sycophantic Ape

Skipping to the point here. People can be made to feel good about things of themselves they are not sure of.

How to Make Someone Love You: Tell Them Something Wonderful About Themselves They Normally Doubt Is True

They will feel good, because the thing they would want to believe, the thing that would make them see themselves positively, the thing that would feed their slanted bias toward themselves … . Ok, I'll finally use the word: The thing that would prop up and feed a person's "ego" or the belief in one's goodness, superiority, and so on, in a world of so many others, well that makes one feel good, whether it is true or not.

So, we see that the intention of this pathetic public pronouncing of a superior human will to live is to salve the egos of the masses. Why does it feel good? Because it is universally true that the ego is in constant assault from something which makes it feel not good.

What is that thing that makes people feel not good about themselves, so that being told something that counters that would make them feel good? Well, the answers, by psychologists since Freud, have many terms attached to them. And by the way, before the psychologists there were the theologians attempting to answer this. But Freud's analysis not only answered it, but put it in the largest context possible — one into which both psychologists and theologians would find an inroad.

We can say, to backtrack a bit, that this pandering by those in front of audiences makes people feel good because it supports the defense system that all humans have erected against the real truth — that zeitgeist-shattering one that Freud was first to fully explicate. It feels good because it supports the denial that all humans have against the real truth that they feel about themselves, one of the things that human societies universally consign to that black hole of the *Unapproved and Hidden.*[1]

"Quit Hitting Yourself!"

So this repetitive obvious truth about humans having a strong Will to Live is repeated to please audiences and make them feel good — "people-pleasing" — because it is a salve to the egos of the masses, which in reality are not merely bruised. No, this goes directly toward propping up a particular defense, a particular denial that we all carry. And that denial is that, IN TRUTH, humans don't at all feel like they have a tremendous Will to Live. How can I say that? Well, how many things do you know you do which are "not good for you"? How many things do you not do which you know would aid the cause of our supposed universal desire to Live and to Live as long as possible?

The point is that humans, along with a Will to Life that is undeniable, also have a Will to Death.

How many times have you woken up, thought about all the pressures and obligations, or complexities, responsibilities ... . thought about all the seemingly insurmountable obstacles or challenges that you are facing ... thought about all the things that just have to get done, yet you feel that you could not possibly have the time to do all of them.... How many times have you woken up and felt overwhelmed with what life has become and not wished to just curl up, go back to sleep, and never wake up again? How many times have you taken to drugs or intoxicants in full knowledge of their negative and even dire concomitants and simply thought to yourself, "Aw, what the hell. If I were to die, so what? What's so great about life anyway?" Or, with less clarity, simply said, "Well nobody lives forever!"

Do they sound like the pronouncements of a species that has a tremendous will to live? No, in fact, alongside our Will to Live, we have not only a Will to Die, but even a will to self-destruction.

Right about now, it might be occurring to you how *this makes sense of so much, seemingly insane, human behavior we've seen of late. This Will to Die explains why we continue nonchalantly our march to armageddon. It shines light on how we can suck up air in cities that gives us raging allergies, clogs our lungs as bad as chronic smoking would, and will kill off the children we raise there long before their times. It reveals how we could drink poisoned water, blithely go about our business as the globe fills up with nuclear radiation and makes its way into our food supplies and as our government refuses even to test for it, and turn our backs as the oceans die, and killer tornadoes, hurricanes, earthquakes, and tsunamis chalk up thousands in the kill column. It explains why people allow themselves to be enslaved and controlled by others — allowing fascism in established democracies — unconcernedly voting for rabid folk who would take away their rights and security and bring down their freedoms, health, and even lives, while watching those living under totalitarian systems* risk *their lives for such freedom and rights and democracy. So much more.*

But anyway….

Suicidal Ape

Now, the intention here is not to repeat all that Freud and psychologists have said in showing how this works. Besides, just look at the evidence around you of addiction, chronic accidentalism, unhealthy behavior habits without number, and of course the ultimate evidence: suicide.

And by the way, if we have such a strong Will to Live, superior to all other species, then explain why it is so that we are the only species that has suicide? And we're supposed to be the conscious ones?

What Freud pointed out has tremendous explanatory power, especially now in our current worldwide financial upheaval, depression/recession, expanding global fascism, nuclear meltdowns, oil spills, near environmental collapse, wars and terrorism, nuclear armaments of planetary annihilation, and tendency to pollute body as well as environment, and even to do it thoughtlessly, in full knowledge of the consequences.

The Only Important Question and About That Inner Monster of Yours

I repeat: Freud established that we act out a will to live and to be in the sun and to have fun and to love and to like goodness and health and truth.

I repeat: Freud also saw we have at other times an opposite feeling which causes us to want to live in the dark — to not be around people, to shy away from life and the light and being seen and recognized and even to wanting to be lonely — that causes us to not care about fun, to hate and be angry, indeed to hate everyone and even to want to lash out at them for no reason other than what might be self-labeled as spite; that causes us to hate goodness, calling things "kumbaya moments," that causes us to be jealous of others who are more giving and to hate them for that, call people "goody two-shoes" or saying something is "schmaltzy"; or saying that all that good stuff is just "drama"; and putting out terms like "bleeding heart" liberals; that causes us to beat up on our bodies and abuse them with all kinds of substances and behaviors; and that causes us to not care about the truth, but rather to say things instead to hurt, get revenge, to get back at; or to say untruths to get advantage, to disable our competitors, to hide from the evils we commit which enslave us further in the hiding of them, and so much more.

Pandavas Versus Kauravas

Epic Struggle, Good Versus Evil, Depicted in *Bhagavad Gita*

Freud said we struggled between these two opposite feelings throughout our lives. It is because of this contradiction we carry inside that we can never be truly sure of who we are and even that we can question our motives and intentions (those more self-analytical of us). It is because of this contradiction that we can always feel we could have done better, that people don't know everything about us, even when they say they do, and that sometimes we fear, especially when we are younger, that if people knew what we had inside they would shy away, not like us, think us to be bad, even monstrous.

By the Way, About That Inner Monster of Yours....

It is because of this contradiction that people are so terrified of revealing themselves, lest some of that not socially appropriate, not socially sanctioned, not socially approved part of themselves slip out. And the fear there is that then we will be seen to have been found out; and that then we will be confirmed in our worst fears that indeed that "other" part of ourselves is — the horror that cannot even be spoken in one's mind — that dark part of ourselves is the *real* us ... which carries with it the view that any of the "good" in us is just a cover up so that other people will not know.

Mask on a Monster, Lipstick on a Pig

But Freud took it beyond our inner struggles and talked about how the events of the world, the actions and movements of history, the dramas of all the ages, are in fact the products of this inner struggle. Desperate between these poles, we join together with others of the same feeling — whether of lightness or of negativity — in multiple relations and groups on both sides of that struggle. More than that, while driven unwittingly from sources on one side, we expend ourselves in complex ways, in concert with these other, to represent these groups as well as ourselves as acting out from sources on the other side; we mask ourselves as the other.

Babel's Inner Blueprint

Ultimately, these groups magnify our powers. And the cumulative acts of many individuals, along with the actions of groups and their leaders, all within complex and contradictory motives at all levels and in every matter, create the complex events of all times. All these happenings are at base the story of inner conflicts — complex outer conflicts notwithstanding. In a cumulative manner and over time, things are ever more convoluted and twisted and complicated through the actions of the myriad characters — all of whom conflicted inside, act inconsistently, and out of their own unique struggles which have all of us perceiving and interpreting things in ways totally unique to ourselves.

Again, The Question

These huge world events, then, Freud laid at the feet of the individual struggle. Basically the world becomes an arena of the acting of the Will to Life against the Will to Death, of Eros versus Thanatos.

That is why I say what we are discussing is an age-old question. Although to our detriment ... or fortune? ... it is now more than any other time crucially relevant, and it is of the most immense importance and consequence as to the winner of that inner struggle.

For while we watched with paralyzed hand on one side, on the other our lesser selves are presently taking us on a path that leads inevitably, one way or another, to total species extinction. And not just that alone, but in fact total life extinction on this planet, and possibly even to planetary annihilation — the destruction of this planet itself.

That is why in the book that follows this one in the Return to Grace series I focus on this question of dire importance. In *Apocalypse NO, Apocalypse or Earth Rebirth and the Emerging Perinatal Unconscious,* I talk more about this Will to Death manifesting currently as planetary suicide. But unlike Freud I do not address this Will to Death in a general sense. I deal specifically with its existence as an element of the current struggle between those of us who would live and those opposing that.

I deal with the question of the sway of the "dark side" as over against the Power of Truth, Love, Higher Power; God ... if you will; Sathya Sai, that is, Truth Love ... if you will; the Universe; or simply the Better Angels of Our Nature manifesting in increasing numbers of lives....

The questions we need to ask are about which side will win in the end. For certainly it will be decided one way or the other, and soon, of that we can be sure. And that is what makes this time and this question different from any other time. Because this question is not an academic one, now. It is one whose answer will become known far sooner than we would ever wish.

So, we will continue to live, and we will become good citizens of this planet and our species will continue on?

True? False?

This discussion is only now beginning.

EPILOGUE

APOCALYPSE – NO!

APOCALYPSE OR EARTH REBIRTH AND THE EMERGING PERINATAL UNCONSCIOUS

These are the strangest of days. We live in a time in which ending our species in our lifetime, even eliminating all life on this planet, are very real possibilities. The awareness of this acceleration toward an "end of days" — while so horrifying that we are in denial of it and hardly speak it — hangs over us and affects us in ways singular and fantastic.

The book that follows this one in the Return to Grace series, Volume 4 — *Apocalypse NO, Apocalypse or Earth Rebirth and the Emerging Perinatal Unconscious* — awakens us to the unique character of our times. There are powerful factors and unconscious influences erupting into our world now which are changing the Earth and us in radical ways ... for good and ill. This unprecedented era in history is rife with the perinatal, that is, with repressed memories locked into us arising from our experiences of birth. We see that our impending apocalypse has to do with birth feelings, birth trauma — an emerging perinatal unconscious.[1]

Herein is revealed the underbelly of our modern world and life and the impetus behind our self-destruction. We see primal forces arising and exposed. We begin to understand how and why this is happening now. Knowing this gives us the power to do something about our dire situation. Finally, we can direct our attention to the roots of our drive to apocalypse and reverse it.

More than that, this awakening provides a way of transformation for ourselves. For we see that in the heart of this darkness we are bringing down upon us lies the most incredible opportunity for taking a leap beyond what we think of as human nature. This time calls for a new hero's cycle — one that leaves behind the thuggishness of the old one. We are lifted beyond ourselves in a higher calling and a transcendent yet deeply rooted spirituality.

We realize that the necessary answer to the dilemma of apocalypse or Earth rebirth lies, not only in the resurrection of a new Earth, but in the dawning of a new self as well.

We will either heroically, somehow, save our species and our planet, which will require a change of our human nature unlike anything that has been asked of our species ever before; or we will be witnesses to the elimination of life on this planet in some way that we cannot imagine but can only be horrific in the extreme. This book is about facing, not denying, the uniquely dire character of our times and finding out what it says about us and requires of us.

There is much here to see, and so much of it the mainstream would never touch for fear of creating a panic. Still, to survive our species must face our problems, not look away. And there is a nobility in doing that, which is unlike any kind of nobility or heroism required of us previously.

However, this time brings with it an advantage and opportunity also unprecedented: At no other time has a higher calling or a path of true nobility of soul been more visible. To align oneself with this cause lifts one out of oneself and one's petty concerns into a heady and invigorating life purpose. There is great likelihood that we will be unable to reverse our dire trajectory; that is true. Still, those who face and take up this challenge will not suffer the agony of regretting that one could have done something but did not.

Though we will need many noble souls to reverse our current downslide into oblivion, it is possible that simply a significant fraction of the world's population — like the "leaven in the dough" — can make all the difference in the world, literally, by tipping our course one way as opposed to another. This is especially true if such people — because of their healing and their awareness of the crisis — are motivated to place themselves in positions of influence and education, or to put their efforts toward healing, on individual and collective levels, in larger numbers than the average populace would. We can be heroes, standing in the right place and with the lever big enough, who move the world.

NOTES

Chapter One

1. While the severity/seriousness of our predicament is considerably watered-down and glossed over for the sake of consumption in the following report, it is instructive nevertheless. It shows the extent to which our precarious situation is known — and even communicated among the educated — albeit in a manner as to not threaten or scare the audience (into action to stop it!):

Has Earth's Sixth Mass Extinction Already Arrived?

ScienceDaily (Mar. 5, 2011) — With the steep decline in populations of many animal species, from frogs and fish to tigers, some scientists have warned that Earth is on the brink of a mass extinction like those that occurred only five times before during the past 540 million years.

Each of these 'Big Five' saw three-quarters or more of all animal species go extinct.

2. In March of 2011, I was sitting in a doctor's waiting room and watching CNN reporting on the Fukushima reactor developments. I heard the following "religious" viewpoint from a stranger who was also watching. We agreed on the magnitude and severity of

this Fukushima event and that of the Gulf Spill, among others. We agreed even on the cause of such events and the way we are being misinformed on them — partly as patronizing misdirection, partly as cover-up. But where we disagreed was on whether it was important or not to do anything about them. As he put it, in his superior but cynical tone, "What can you do? We can't do anything about it, besides it doesn't matter anyway, it's not THIS that is important ... but only after death," pointing heavenward at that. (*sigh*)

3. On the subject of not being able to handle such a huge concept as mass extinction, my correspondent phrased it this way:

The psychology of tragedy — Extinction? I'm afraid haven't got time for it.

Mar 20, 2010 2:18pm by Open Intelligence. "The economy works by making people selfish. Mass extinction is merely collateral damage."

The link shared — to an article by Simon Barnes writing for The Sunday Times, *of London, on March 20, 2010 — reads:*

> *Species are going extinct because humans can't see it happening, and therefore we can't believe it is happening. It is as simple as that.*
>
> *Believing that the elephant will no longer be around is like believing that one day the sun will rise in the west and the stars will fall as rain.*
>
> *We can only really get a handle on the short-term. A generation at most. Long-term planning means the next year or two. Our minds can't cope with anything longer. That's why we choose to govern ourselves by means of a comfortable timescale. Four years, five years: that's Politician's Time.*
>
> *Extinction is a happening thing, as I have pointed out more than once before. But it is happening in slow motion: you don't see a*

monkey turn into a man, and you don't see an animal go extinct. It's just that one day you notice that they haven't been about for a few years. The current rate of extinction is one species an hour....

4. The idea that there was no other time where any human lived knowing of the very real possibility of ending our species in its lifetime was criticized as follows:

No other time has been like this, but there have been plenty of times in the history of the human species where we have been met with the ability to and possibility of our ending — from when we were a few dozen leaving the mythological savanna of Eden to the discovery of the forging of Bronze to the hypothetical Event that led to the Dark Ages, the Apocalypse has been Nigh. It ain't happened yet.

I responded: I have no idea of what time in our evolution that, other than modern times, our species even knew that it was a limited species on a limited globe and had any idea that its actions could wipe out what it thought of as itself as a species, since we did not conceive of ourselves as a limited species in any of those time you speak of. We, with our science and technology are able to know of those times in the past and ourselves. But hell, only in the last five hundred years did we find out we lived on a globe or lived in a solar system! Before that how could anyone in any culture know where either their ability to roam ended or their species no longer existed!

So you miss the point, which is, "no other time" did humans live "KNOWING" that THEY could bring, not only themselves, their families, or their cultures to an end but also THEIR ENTIRE "SPECIES," to an end "in" ... their "lifetime" (not to mention the other estimated 500 million species).

Chapter Two

1. I am not new to this issue, nor have I been lax in trying to do

something about it. I have engaged in considerable activism on a number of issues related to peace, justice, and the environment, particularly the problem of nuclear power. Working as a political activist with Oregon Fair Share in the early Eighties — out of their Springfield, Oregon office — I was one of the score or so involved in the actions that led to ending nuclear plant construction in the entire United States.

I wrote a considerable amount on this subject of the environmental crisis in the Nineties, including at least one online book directly taking up the topic titled *Apocalypse, Or New Age?* Another book, available online, *Primal Renaissance: The Emerging Millennial Return* is extremely important to this topic, and *Falls From Grace*, which is a published thesis as well as online book, is also relevant. I began my first website in 1997 to help with our environmental problems; it is titled *Primal Spirit*. It is no coincidence that at that time, the Nineties, we had a Democrat in the White House.

But since Obama has come into office I have once again been avid in applying my efforts to this all-important issue. I put up a number of websites and blogs to help raise awareness on this and related topics. Among the more important of these are *Apocalypse- No* ; *Culture War, Class War*; and *The Great Reveal by the Planetmates*. I've been expressing these ideas in blogs. *Obvious Unspoken Things, Things That Want to Be Said*, and *Becoming Authentic* are among the most developed of those.

I have been quite active, over the last five years, tweeting and posting about this and related topics on Facebook and Twitter. As an aside, on Facebook, if you are concerned as well, I encourage you to join my group, Planetmate Views there.

These, in addition to youtube videos and audio clips and other productions and projects are indications I have been walking my talk.

Finally, and most importantly, another book of mine is coming out at this time, and it can serve as a companion book or, better, a book that follows from this one. It is titled *Apocalypse NO, Apocalypse or Earth Rebirth and the Emerging Perinatal Unconscious.* These two — *Apocalypse Emergency* and *Apocalypse NO* — are among the ten so far that are in the Return to Grace series of books, which will all be published in the next year or so. All of them, together, represent my efforts to channel my concern for the planet and my love of the many beings on it into constructive action to help protect them and us all. They are the way I am trying to be part of the solution, rather than the problem, in the face of this most dire threat of all time.

2. To glimpse the unimaginable future past the time that we kill off ourselves and all life on this planet and become like Mars, I offer this fantasy around a musical scrap, which is shared on-line:

It is a Requiem for Earth, a metaphysical view, an eerie emotional raw sound. It is sung by two of the last survivors of Earth — from all appearances it would have been the composer SM Adzema and his beloved wife, Mary Lynn Adzema — obviously not professional singers — but heartfelt nonetheless, giving us a glimpse into the profound sadness that must have hung over those last survivors after it became clear that Earth's ecological balance so shattered, there would be no life at all to survive the strange behaviors of what Earthologists have begun calling "the suicidal ape" — referring to the species that alone brought down the entire planet.

Indeed this song, as an electronic scrap mixed in with an island of Earth debris discovered by spacepreuners hurtling swiftly through the Verse not far from the star system's outer reach — the one that had once contained the fabled Earth — is one of the few very rare looks into the hearts and minds of those people as they watched, helplessly, as their planet's delicate life sheath imploded with a gathering rapidity. Some who have heard this musical scrap claim that it supports the more radical theory of this event of a planet murder-suicide — the theory that the suicidal ape was divided on this global murder-suicide, with a goodly number of this species working furiously to save the planet even as stronger, more powerful forces, for reasons still not understood, continued their secretive sabotage of the other side's efforts, ensuring the downfall of all, including the saboteurs themselves.

At first hearing, this song seems to be expressing an awareness of the sadness that would accompany such a horrific event, at odds with the stories of "suicide ape's" gleeful festive behavior in the midst of the massive killing and suicide.

3. An example of this came out in the wake of the Fukushima reactor blow-ups. Republicans said a number of stupid and insensitive things, which were widely shared and roundly ridiculed. Among those tidbits of foolery was Ann Coulter's public statement that "Radiation is good for you." Ann Coulter: "Radiation Is Good For You" at http://front.moveon.org/ann-coulter-radiation-is-good-for-you/?rc=fb.fan

4. I have presented much of the information in this book and its companion book, *Apocalypse NO*, at conferences, beginning in the mid-Nineties. Some of the material has been published in printed professional journals. And earlier versions of this piece have been posted on these sites, *Apocalypse Emergency, Primal Spirit, Apocalypse - No!,* and *Things That Want to Be Said* — of those sites which are still in existence. The unrevised version of this book's companion book, *Apocalypse NO*, titled *Apocalypse, or New Age?* was published in 1999 online and is still at http://www.primalspirit.com/emerging_perinatal_book.htm as of this writing.

Chapter Four

1. See the next chapter — "Chapter Five: Thanatos Walking and the Only Question" — on Freud's view of The Will to Die or *Thanatos,* as he also called it.

2. See the relevant part of the movie, *Zietgeist,* also.

3. See the online article, "Good … God! Hell … No! Recalling the Riotous, Exciting First Days," and the youtube video and online audio, "Breaking News: Hell Doesn't Exist" and the larger audiocast from which "Breaking News" is clipped, "The Great Reveal: Recalling the Riotous, Exciting First Days." I wrote these pieces, and I perform them along with my wife, Mary Lynn Adzema.

4. Getting "breathing holes" and "thinking they are happy" are references to the song, "Sad," by Nirvana. That is a rare song by Kurt Cobain and Nirvana titled, also, "Verse Chorus Verse" … also known as "Sappy." These are the lyrics:

And if you say your prayers
You will make God happy
And if you do what's true\told
You will make me happy
I'll keep you in a jar
And you will seem happy
I'll give you breathing holes
You will think you're happy, now

You're really in a laundry room
You're really in a laundry room
You're really in a laundry room

And if you save yourself
You will make Him happy
He'll bring you fine rewards
Then you will feel happy
I'll keep you in my room
I'm sure you'll be happy
And if you save your soul
You will think you're happy, now

You're really in a laundry room
You're really in a laundry room

You're really in a laundry room
You're really in a laundry room

And if you kill yourself,
You will make him happy
And if you save yourself
Then you will make him happy

He'll keep you in a jar
And you'll think you're happy
He'll give you breathing holes
Then you'll think you're happy

He'll cover you with grass
And you'll think you're happy
Now

You're really in a laundry room,
You're really in a laundry room
The clues that came to you, oh … .

And if you cut yourself
You will think you're happy
He'll keep you in a jar
Then you'll make him happy

He'll give you breathing holes
Then you'll think you're happy
He'll cover you with grass
Then you'll think you're happy
Now

You're really in a laundry room,
You're really in a laundry room
Conclusion came to you, oh … .. (x2)

And if you fool yourself

You will make him happy
He'll keep you in a jar
And you'll think you're happy

He'll give you breathing holes
Then you will seem happy
You'll wallow in your shit
Then you'll think you're happy
Now

You're really in a laundry room (x3)
Conclusion came to you, oh ... ...

5. I just realized that I cannot call our planetmates "animals" anymore. It strikes me as being very much like using the N-word for African-Americans or the Q-word for Gays. For we all know that the word, *animal,* has connotations that are not positive, in fact they are derogatory and demeaning. The word is used as an insult. It does not connote the noble, esteemed but simply different, interesting nature of these conscious souls in relation to us, in truth.

Is it not time we all started referring to our differently embodied brothers and sisters, not as "animals," but as *planetmates* — the ones who we are sharing this planet with, nothing more ... nothing less?

6. See also, in this regard, Fromm's *The Sane Society,* Marx on religion as being the "opiate of the masses," and Sigmund Freud's writings on the role of religion in society as a defense mechanism, especially his *The Future of an Illusion* and *Civilization and Its Discontents.*

7. It is significant that in *The Lord of the Rings* trilogy the power of the Ring, which is a symbol for an all-encompassing untrue belief system that provides comfort, esteem, and well-being — thus an aspect of ego — that the power of the Ring is magnified when it is used. This is equivalent to the assertion, saying out loud of one's

untruths, unrealities … the struggle to find external justification and reinforcement for one's chosen psychotic reality and thus the active enslaving or imprisoning of oneself, in other words, becoming a Gollum.

See also my article on the *Primal Spirit* site, "The Lord of the Rings, Ego, and Addiction."

Chapter Five

1. The "Unapproved and Hidden" is discussed in the chapter, "The First Prasad," in my book, *The Great Reveal by the Planetmates.* The planetmates describe the origins of this tendency of ours to need to speak out our supposed specialness, tying it to our creation of the *Unapproved and Hidden* in societies.

Epilogue

1. For those who wish to continue along on this topic, the book which follows this in the series, Return to Grace, picks up from here, going deeper into the topic … exploring and elaborating and revealing solutions. That book is *Apocalypse NO, Apocalypse or Earth Rebirth and the Emerging Perinatal Unconscious* … available from all major outlets and in electronic or print format.

For those who wish to look into the political and societal aspects of this issue, the book that precedes this one in the Return to Grace series, *Culture War, Class War: Occupy Generations and the Rise and Fall of "Obvious Truths"* is relevant. It, also, is available in print and electronic format.

ABOUT THE AUTHOR

My name is Michael Adzema. I am an environmental activist, writer, primal therapist, breathwork facilitator, and independent scholar.

I have engaged in considerable activism on a number of issues related to peace, justice, and the environment, particularly the problem of nuclear power. Working as an activist with Oregon Fair Share in the early Eighties, I was one of the score or so involved in the actions that led to ending nuclear plant construction in the entire United States. Working out of the Springfield, Oregon office, my part was to go door-to-door canvassing every night for a few years in Springfield and in towns up and down the Willamette Valley educating people about the dangers of nuclear power, and weaponry, and the financial scandal of the WPPPS plants being built in Washington state. My reasons for doing this were the apocalyptic danger of nuclear power — which has now been shown to be prophetic with the Fukushima disaster, occurring thirty years after we were warning about such a thing happening in our conversations in people's homes — and the threat to all life on this planet from the existence and proliferation of nuclear weapons.

I worked as canvasser and eventually crew leader and observed how our efforts at education led to folks getting involved, signing petitions, and even the folks of Springfield demonstrating in the streets about these WPPPS plants. Eventually, the organization I worked for, Oregon Fair Share, discovered Springfield law that stipulated that its citizens could not be indebted/taxed over a certain percent without a vote of the people. There had been no vote. The cost overruns of WPPS would have led to indebtedness of approximately $8,000 per household throughout the Northwest — just to "mothball" the plants.

With this in mind, enough grass-roots pressure was brought to bear, which led to a lawsuit, which was taken on, *pro bono*, by Bob

Ackerman, a local attorney. Current US Congressman, Representative Peter DeFazio became involved and helped in the lawsuit. We won, creating the largest bond default in United States history. Other municipalities followed suit. Nuclear power was shown to be the financial gravy train for investors and the financial rip-off for consumers that it is. No application to build a nuclear plant in the entire United States was filed after that.

Surpassing my activist work, however, is my expertise in the fields of prenatal and perinatal psychology, primal psychology, psychohistory, psychological anthropology, and humanistic psychology. I was the first person to teach prenatal and perinatal psychology at the university level, which I did at Sonoma State University in Rohnert Park, California, in the early Nineties. For years I gave sessions in primal therapy, rebirthing, and breathwork, and I conducted two-to-three-day workshops, with my wife, Mary Lynn Adzema, in primal breathwork out of our facility as well as at professional conferences. My book, *Falls from Grace*, is listed as a reference in the field of prenatal and perinatal psychology on *Wikipedia*. I served as editor and publisher of the professional journal *Primal Renaissance: The Journal of Primal Psychology*, which was at one time put out by the International Primal Association.

I have done considerable work in these fields as well: economics, anthropology, history, and environmental studies. As an undergraduate in the early Seventies, my studies focused on humanistic psychology at Franklin and Marshall College. I received a degree in humanistic psychology from the University of Colorado at Denver in 1979. I did doctoral work in psychological anthropology at the University of California, San Diego. I received an interdisciplinary M.A. — psychology, anthropology, philosophy, history — from Sonoma State University in Prenatal and Perinatal Psychology in 1994.

Most of my life I have spent in writing, teaching, facilitating, and research.

Things I take pride in: all of my writings; any way I have helped clients in therapy; any way I have helped students when I taught at the universities; my websites and blogs, the fact that I was a hippie and a young radical and antiwar activist in the Sixties; the fact that I lived during the incredible Sixties and got to experience and get bitten by the idealism and global visionary bug, which I hold fast, to this day; and the fact that I was the perfect age to understand and experience it — in my late teens and early twenties; the fact that I had the sense and courage to do thorough primal therapy in Denver during the years 1975–1980; my wife, Mary Lynn, and my family.

My main mission in life: Searching for truth in a world of Lies, Liars; wanting to help as we kill the planet, all of us, all our children, grandchildren, and all the planetmates, all the beings, of which God made millions of species, who have lived and had a home on this planet until only lately, the planet-killing half-borns, the species, *Homo sapiens*, evolved, to the extreme detriment of the millions of other planetmates.

Damn good example of why you should get references, always, before allowing anyone to move in.